Contents

PREFACE

The central topic of this Nordic SADC Journalism Centre course component is ethics and journalism. We will focus upon some of the key questions regarding ethical responsibilities and rights in the media in general and journalism in particular. It is through critical reflection upon what legitimately may be demanded of the media, in terms of duties and responsibilities, that it is possible to reach some form of agreement on what the ethical standards of media practices should be. I hope that the issues raised here will lead to discussions in all the courses run by the centre.

The following text is based on many sources. Partly it takes its point of departure from several books and articles published over the previous decade or so on the topic of media ethics, and partly it is based on research on and text about the media situation in southern Africa that has been undertaken by the author.

Some texts have been more important than others in developing this introduction to media ethics. They are acknowledged in the endnotes, but it is necessary to mention some of them here as they have not only been essential for the working out of the principled arguments, but also examples, formulations and paragraphs from these works are to be found here almost verbatim. The most important of these inspirations has been the introduction to the bibliography of *Media Ethics*[1] by Barrie MacDonald and Michel Petheram. Other important contributions are several articles in the special issue on media ethics of *The European Journal of Communication*[2] edited by Kaarle Nordenstreng. Andrew Belsey and Ruth Chadwick have edited an extremely interesting book, *Ethical Issues in Journalism and the Media*[3]; as has Matthew Kieran[4]. An important Scandinavian contribution is *Journalistikens etiska problem*[5] by Mats Ekström and Stig Arne Norhstedt; and John Wilson has written an engaging and very useful, principled and practical guide to issues in journalism[6] relevant to the ethical debate.

Media Ethics

An introduction and overview

Nordic SADC Journalism Centre

Helge Rønning
Professor of Media and Communication
University of Oslo, Norway

Teacher's Guide

Francis P. Kasoma
Professor of Journalism and Mass Communication
University of Zambia

ETHICS, MEDIA AND JOURNALISM

Broadly understood, ethics[7] deals with all the factors that play a role in human life and interaction between individuals, and the individual and society. It is about how we should live our lives. Thus, it is a question of daily life and of philosophy. Ethics has played an extremely important part in the history of philosophy. In the Western tradition, it covers thinkers from Aristotle, to Immanuel Kant, to John Rawls. It is central to religious philosophy in all cultures, and the African concept of *ubuntu,* dealing with human compassion and communal togetherness, clearly falls within the range of ethical philosophy.

(Ethics focuses on how one decides what is right or wrong, fair or unfair, caring or uncaring, good or bad, responsible or irresponsible[8]) Ethics applies to issues of virtues and vices, and questions basic principles and rules in the evaluation of human conduct and social relations. It is concerned with both character and conduct. Ethics deals with what is often characterised as moral concepts. These change from culture to culture and their application to complex situations is often anything but clear. Some basic concepts may be a source of conflict – for example, when we have to choose between being fair to an individual or a small group on the one hand and serving the general good of, say, an entire community, on the other.

Understood as the systematic study of morality, ethics examines basic moral attitudes, dispositions, beliefs, standards, principles, ideals and practices. This involves both clarifying our understanding of these matters and evaluating their merits. Ethics refers to the study of a vast range of practical concerns of which people often have a certain intuitive grasp, but are often not clearly understood and subject to controversy. It deals with the values people actually accept, and those that they ought to accept. The first aspect is empirical, or descriptive. The study of morality can tell us what particular moral values a particular group of people accept. The second aspect is normative, and concerned with determining what values are worthy of our acceptance.

Asking whether an act is ethical or unethical elicits a 'yes' or 'no' response, and the ensuing discussion is immediately cast in a two-value framework. However, asking the question 'How ethical is it?' elicits statements about a degree of ethical quality, including highly ethical, moderately ethical, slightly ethical, neutral, slightly unethical, moderately unethical, or highly unethical. There is also a vast range of concepts typically associated with ethics and morality, such as what is fair/unfair, considerate/inconsiderate, caring/uncaring, humane/inhumane, and respectful/disrespectful.

Ethics also sometimes refers to specific sets of principles, standards and ideals embraced by individuals or particular groups or organisations. We may refer to someone's personal ethics, to the ethics of a social group (for example, a religious sect), or a code of ethics of a professional organisation, a business, or a government body. Thus, the study of ethics includes personal ethics, codes of ethics, personal morality and moral codes. In relation to the media, all of these aspects are in some way relevant, even if the focus is on mediated communication rather than ethics in general. Ethical issues are potentially relevant to any of the variables included in typical communication models: the source or sender; the message or content; channels of communication; receivers; the effects; and the situation, environment, or context of communication.

The rapid political and technological changes in the media and communications have raised many fundamental issues that extend beyond journalism, but are central to the question of what journalistic ethics entail. In this book, we will deal with ethics and the media in a wider sense, but concentrate on ethical challenges to the news media. Given this perspective, it is impossible not to touch upon what should be done in communications; how information, news and culture ought to be produced and distributed; and how changes in the world of communications interact with the rights and duties of the various actors and institutions in the media arena.

The media have a strong and multifaceted influence upon how we understand and shape the societies in which we live. The media provide us with news and views, transmitted by means of reporting and investigative journalism, information and entertainment. The media contribute to our understanding of the world, but they often distort rather than provide the truth. The media engage with and affect our beliefs, values and commitments. Given the media's increasing presence and influence throughout the world, many ethical and social questions are raised that need to be addressed, both by the media practitioners and by the public. This has resulted in an increasingly important public debate about media and ethics. In most cases, the background to these debates has been public outrage against media content and actions. Accusations of bias, cynicism, manipulation, intrusions into privacy, and worries about the damaging or distorting effect of television have been among the issues raised. Invariably, they have led to discussions about possible forms of media regulation or censorship, as well as the appropriateness of libel laws.

Media ethics is also concerned with the problems that media practitioners have to face as they go about their work. While these problems affect all media, they also influence culture and politics in a wider context. Media ethics is sometimes considered a branch of applied ethics, which implies investigations in moral philosophy. Because it also raises questions of rights and politics, it can also be considered a part of social philosophy, sociology, political science, history and psychology. However, first and foremost, it is linked to media practices of all kinds. When we discuss the media, we first think of journalists and reporters, then those about whom the journalists write, who are also those who read, hear or see the media – the public. Traditionally, journalistic ethics is linked to the press, but the news media of today consist of radio and television, and increasingly the World Wide Web. Media ethics is also important beyond news media; they pertain to entertainment media and formats – fiction, documentaries and semi-fiction in drama, films, magazines, etc. In daily practice, we do not discuss media ethics in a principled philosophical way, but rather from a practical point of view. Media ethics is usually encountered at an individual level. Did a certain report constitute an invasion of privacy? Was the article libellous? Was the government justified in withholding a particular piece of information? Is this film immoral? Is violence on television harmful?

Journalistic ethics may, despite variances based on different historical and cultural contexts, be said to constitute some universally accepted basic elements of concern. These have been identified as: the quest for truth, an aspiration for responsibility, and a dedication to the principle of free expression. These universals are interpreted differently in different circumstances. For example, truth in many contexts may be understood as authenticity in a social context rather than as strict correspondence to static reality. Media ethics thus raises the dilemma of universal versus particular values. Again, this may be linked to other intellectual challenges of a general nature. The first of these is the dilemma of individualism versus collectivism. While ethics, by its very nature, invites us to consider an individual conscience, we must refer to the social and community setting of the individual, which is central to problems of citizenry and democracy, and are linked to the important ethical question of journalistic accountability.

A dilemma raised by institutionalising ethical rules for the media is that of regulation. The adoption of professional ethics and the setting up of regulatory bodies by media practitioners are typically seen as substitutes for official government regulation. Nevertheless, self-regulation is also a form of regulation and pertains to the question of freedom versus control. All attempts to institutionalise media ethics involve mediating accountability between the gatekeepers and other actors in the communication process.

Journalistic ethics ... the quest for truth, an aspiration for responsibility, and a dedication to the principle of free expression.

A question that is almost invariably raised when one discusses journalism and ethics is: Which and whose ethics? Does it make sense to think we can make ethical demands of journalism, a practice that always seems to involve muckraking, one-sidedness, deceit, dependency on rumours, intrusions into privacy etc.?

Perhaps it is unreasonable to demand ethical, professional standards from journalists. Maybe the profession operates on the basis of standards that are different from those that exist in ordinary life, such as honesty and a duty to tell the truth? Maybe the entertainment function of journalism is more important than the information function? This leads to other ethical standards. Certainly, in some forms of popular journalism in the West, this has been maintained as a reason for publishing stories that go against ordinarily accepted forms of journalistic ethics. It has also led to modern popular journalism being held in rather low esteem. A typical pronouncement along these lines would be: 'Journalists are not the bearers, but the whores of conscience.'

Because the media hold such a central place in the democratic process, and have become an increasingly important economic factor, it is necessary to emphasise the responsibilities of the media. Their obligations and their specific rights arise out of their special function in the democratic process. Unethical journalistic activity will undermine the public's trust and, with that, the democratic and representative function of the news media.

A HISTORICAL PERSPECTIVE

The discussion about norms and ethics, journalism and the transmission of news is as old as the press itself, and, in many ways, it has its roots in societies where information was transmitted by word of mouth. The question of truth in what is mediated was, and is, important in oral societies. It is easy to forget this when we discuss ethics of news and storytelling, because we are so used to linking it to the modern media situation of newspapers, radio, television and the Internet. It is also important to bear in mind that the modern media are dependent on stories often told by word of mouth, particularly so in Africa. The questions of whether journalism has as its goal to inform or to entertain, to tell the truth or to tell a good story, is linked to the question of storytelling, and to the problem of the relationship between what is being told and the subject with which the narrative deals.

Since the early examples (mid 16th century) of a press in Europe, which was distributed in marketplaces, and often covered sensational, gruesome tales, through to the later, more sombre, newssheets dealing with trade and commerce, journalism has been caught in the dilemma that it is simultaneously there to entertain and to inform. One of the more frequent criticisms levelled at the press is that it allows the entertainment function to count more than the information function. Since the earliest history of the press, there have been three actors in the struggle for defining its role: the publishers and the journalists, the audience, and the authorities. These three have always pursued different, if not opposing interests.

Journalists and publishers have always had both ideal and material reasons for publishing newspapers. To present news and information, and create a public opinion have been regarded as important, but to succeed in this, there has always existed a need for an audience who will buy the newspapers and find them entertaining. The larger the audience, the more important the message of the newspaper – but also the more publishers will earn from their sales. Publishers and journalists must satisfy the needs of their audience, the public: information about all kinds of things – social events, politics, economy, entertainment – including rumours and tales of the unusual.

The public has, of course, never been a homogenous entity. It consists of different groups with different interests, morals and standards. Consequently, the conflict between the press and critical representatives of the public has always existed.

From the beginning, the attitude of the state, political and religious authorities and the power elites to the press was ambivalent. On the one hand, they often used the press to influence opinion, but also reserved the right to censor. Therefore, freedom of expression has always been a central element in the discussion of press ethics.

Censorship has always been intimately linked with the development of media technologies. Highly developed societies are now in the last stages of a process that started with Gutenberg – the struggle between those who wish to use the technologies of dissemination to spread messages, images, information, entertainment and art as freely as possible, and those who, for a variety of reasons, want to control and regulate this dissemination. As Edward Lucie-Smith has put it: '... the means of suppression always ran snapping at the heels of the means of dissemination.'[9]

By looking back at the early history of printing, it is possible to put what is happening now in relation to the new digital media technologies in a historical perspective. The printing and publishing institutions that developed in early modern Europe, and which constitute the first media establishments, were cultural as well as economic, political and religious institutions. They served as a meeting place, as centres in an evolving public sphere, where writers, intellectuals and scholars met, discussed and found ways of disseminating their works and ideas. The relationship between the early publishers and the writers who provided them with their manuscripts, and religious and political authorities, was an uneasy one. Printed material had the potential of challenging the symbolic order of the Church and the absolutist State, and both the State and the Church sought to both use and control the new printing industry. In spite of attempts to suppress texts that were deemed dangerous, immoral, heretic, etc., it proved difficult to ban and censor books, journals and newspapers. The printers, often at great risks to themselves, found ways to evade censorship in one country by printing in other, more liberal environments, and having printed material smuggled across the borders. One could say that, paradoxically, censorship then, as later in history, stimulated the trade in banned texts, and challenged the authorities wishing to censor the print medium.

... the printed word came to be a central element in the development of the public sphere ...

From a contemporary, multicultural perspective, it is easy to forget that the practice of censorship and restrictions of the right to express yourself freely in print, and in other media, does not only belong to political systems associated with absolutism and dictatorship, fundamentalism and intolerance. Censorship and other forms of control over the printed word are part of Western development, and have been so up to the early 1960s, in societies that now strongly promulgate freedom of expression. In early modern Western Europe, the authorities, civil and clerical, regarded the printed word with great suspicion and saw the book as a possible vehicle for spreading their points of view, but equally as a means for the distribution of heresy and sedition.

The printed word and its practitioners – printers, publishers and writers – were regarded as part of a new social group pursuing interests that were often contrary to the interests of political and religious authorities. Thus, the printed word came to be a central element in the development of the public sphere, which established itself as separate from the State and the Church in early modern Europe.

It is also worth noting that, in the context of this development, both artistic and non-fictional, argumentative texts were seen as equally powerful and important to the establishment and expression of new structures of feeling that went against absolutism. It is important to always bear in mind that the right to freedom of expression is not a right given forever; it is a right that needs to be defended in a constant struggle.

With the development of the mass popular press in the USA and Europe linked to the growth of a mass market and mass advertising, and at the time voting rights were extended to larger parts of the population, the press came to be part of two systems that continue to create dilemmas for the media: mass consumption and mass democracy. This was also a development that highlighted the moral conflicts which came to exist between a sensationalist press, which did not always take the question of truth and reliable sources seriously, and the critique from the intellectual elites of society of the press for not living up to intellectual standards of objectivity and fairness.

This again led to the belief that press-proprietors, editors and journalists came up with their own forms of ethical self-regulation in order to avoid the State authorities setting the standards. Thus, the development of journalistic codes can be seen as a continuous process where the three main actors – the media-practitioners, the public and the authorities – interact with and influence each other.

THE DEVELOPMENT OF MEDIA IDEOLOGIES

The relationship between the media and the State has been at the centre of many attempts to translate political principles into normative theories of the role of communication in society. The most well-known example may be the typology of press systems presented by Siebert, Peterson and Schramm in *Four Theories of the Press*[10] in 1956, which can be read as an attempt to establish criteria for the evaluation of media systems and as a Cold War defence of a liberal media system. However, the book has clearly dated and has lost much of its relevance. The attempt to set up ideal types of media systems may contribute to a principled understanding of the position of the media in relation to political powers. The book identified four types of media political regimes: an authoritarian regime, a liberal regime, a social responsible system and a Soviet-Communist regime. The political developments in Europe and elsewhere from 1989 onwards rendered the simplistic distinction between liberal and communist regimes obsolete. Since then, no one has launched a new typology of media political regimes at a global level, although Dennis McQuail[11] added more types, namely the development theory type, and the democratic-participant theory, in order to include developments in the Third World, as well as new paradigms in development theory.

Attempts to typologise media systems and the ethical and political implications of these obviously have shortcomings. It is necessary to view them as attempts at creating a form of ideal types for systematising the conditions under which media and the press operate, thus establishing the background to the ethical codes that exist in different societies. One of the most interesting attempts at drawing up systems of communication was made by Raymond Williams[12] in the 1960s. He distinguished between what he called the authoritarian, the paternal, the commercial and the democratic communication systems. The descriptions of these systems should be seen as ideal types, and not as something that exists in reality.

In the authoritarian system, communications are seen as part of the machinery through which a minority governs a society. The first purpose of communication is to transmit the instructions, ideas and attitudes of the ruling group. As a matter of policy, alternative instructions, ideas and attitudes are excluded. A monopoly over the means of communication is a necessary part of the whole political system: only certain printers, publishing houses, newspapers, theatres, broadcasting stations are seen as legitimate. Sometimes these will be directly controlled by the ruling group, which will then directly decide what is transmitted. At other times, control that is more indirect will be completed by a system of censorship, and often by a system of political and administrative action against sources unfavourable to those in power. Brutal dictatorships and military regimes are examples of how this type of system may be implemented. The situation in Malawi under Banda's dictatorship may be used as an example.

A paternal system is an authoritarian system with a conscience – one with values and purposes beyond the maintenance of its own power. Authoritarians, on various grounds, claim the right to rule. In a paternal system, the rulers asserted their duty to protect and guide the masses. This involves the exercise of control, but it is a control directed towards the development of the majority in ways thought desirable by the ruling echelons. If the means of communication is monopolised, it is argued that this prevents the means being abused by groups that are destructive or evil. Censorship is widely used in such a system, both directly and indirectly, and defended because certain groups and individuals need, in their own interest and in the public interest, protection against certain kinds of art or ideas that would be harmful to them. Thus, the controllers of a paternal system see themselves as guardians of what they perceive as the values of the society they control. The paternal system can vary in the degree to which it explicitly announces its role or explains its methods. The actual methods can also vary widely – sometimes being very Draconian or at times allowing a measure of controlled dissent or tolerance as a safety valve. This system resembles the situation that existed in the so-called developmental or socialist one-party states in Africa.

The commercial attitude to communications is powerfully opposed to both authoritarianism and paternalism. Instead of communication being for government or for control, it is argued that citizens have the right to offer for sale any kind of work, and that everyone has the right to buy anything that is offered in the marketplace. In this way, it is claimed that freedom of communication is secured. In its early (and some later) stages, such a system is certainly a means to freedom when compared with either of the former systems. However, since this freedom depends on the market, it can run into difficulties. Practical control of the means of communication, over large areas and particularly of the more expensive kinds, can pass to individuals or groups whose main, if not only, qualification will be that they possess or can raise the necessary capital. Such groups will often be unrepresentative of the society as a whole. Therefore, the control claimed as a matter of power by authoritarians, and as a matter of principle by paternalists, is often achieved as a matter of practice in the operation of the commercial system. Anything can be said, provided you can afford to say it and that you can say it profitably. This is the media ideology often associated with the USA, and to some degree resembles the media situations in Latin American countries.

The democratic system of communication is an ideal, in that it does not exist in its full sense. It shares with the early commercial system a definition of communication that insists that everyone has the right to offer and to receive what he or she chooses. It is firmly against authoritarian control of what can be expressed, and against paternal control of what ought to be expressed. It is also against commercial control of what can profitably be said as this can also be seen as a form of tyranny. The democratic system is founded on two basic rights: the right to transmit and the right to receive. These rights can never be tampered with. If they are ever limited by some majority decision of the society, this can happen only after open and adequate public discussion, to which all are free to contribute. Moreover, such limitations will remain open to challenge and review. On the right to transmit, the basic principle of democracy is that, since all are full members of the society, all have the right to speak as they wish. This is not only an individual right, but also a social need, since democracy depends on the active participation and the free contribution of all its members. The right to receive is complementary to this. It is the means of participation and of common discussion. The institutions necessary to guarantee these freedoms must be of a public service nature, but it is very important that the idea of public service should not be used as a cover for a paternal or even an authoritarian

The democratic system is founded on two basic rights: the right to transmit and the right to receive.

13

system. The idea of public service must be detached from the idea of public monopoly, and remain public service in the true sense. The situation in the Scandinavian countries is the closest one comes to the practical realisation of a democratic media system.

Most media systems in the world have elements of the four types outlined previously, but they are also linked to different historical and political contexts. In some cases, the authoritarian or paternal systems dominate; in others, the commercial system is prominent. An ideal democratic public service system does not exist in a pure form, even if the principles on which it is based play a central role in the struggle to build and defend democracy.

A claim that is sometimes made is that commitment to freedom of speech requires the provision of facilities for speech. Consequently, the public has the right to express opinions in newspaper columns, and to appear on radio and television. Without this access, the public has no real freedom of the press; only those who own the means of communication do. Those who have access to radio, television, newspapers, and magazine and book publishers, have greater ability to speak than those without. It is argued that, as there is no true marketplace of ideas, something should be done (for example, through government action) to rectify the balance and make provisions in the form of subsidies or regulations so that the press and broadcasting services accurately and fairly represent the fullest possible range of opinions and experiences of society.

The argument is based on ideas of freedom as a kind of power, and of democracy as the opportunity for everyone to communicate equally. However, it may be argued that such an interpretation of press freedom is removed from another principle, namely that one of the most important aspect is editorial freedom. If individuals could force their opinions into newspapers, editors would lose their freedom of decision. A further objection is that, in a democracy respecting freedom of expression, no one is prevented by direct governmental coercion from starting a newspaper or magazine, or from publishing a book. They may be prevented by economic considerations from doing so, but this is a different constraint from deprivation by government or other human action. However, many countries have a system of licensing newspapers by the government.

The general view is that the media serve some useful social function, and that is why it must be seen as having a public service function and, in some way, be socially responsible. But how does one define 'useful social function' and 'social responsibility'? This is the foundation of all attempts at defining ethical norms for media performance. Social responsibility theory contends that, since the channels of communication are now so limited, those who own the channels and those who work within them must accept a responsibility to society along with the freedom they enjoy from any government interference. That responsibility is to provide a truthful, balanced and comprehensive account of the news. But who decides what is socially responsible? If it is the government, then freedom is lost. What kinds of sanctions will restrict irresponsible newspapers? The term 'social responsibility' captures the two sides of a classic democratic dilemma: a press free of all constraints could easily run amok in its drive for power and profit; a press that is overly constrained by the power of the State would fail to achieve its mission of informing citizens. Nevertheless, socially responsible media are media in tension, conscious of their obligations to enlighten readers and viewers, and all too aware of their deadlines and competitors.

There is a danger that the concept of social responsibility may be taken over by those with a very narrow view of what is good for society. For example, it has been argued that governments should be engaged in raising the moral quality of the community and therefore must judge and limit public discussion according to the moral quality of the writer or speaker. This could mean, however, that anything critical of existing institutions could be considered as lowering the moral quality of the community. Similarly, it has been argued that oppositional groups have no claim to free expression because they are 'disloyal'. This was, for example, an argument used against anti-apartheid activists in South Africa under the National Party regime. It is an argument that is constantly used against dissident voices in all authoritarian systems.

DEMOCRATIC FUNCTIONS OF THE MEDIA

Graham Murdock[13] has identified the roles of the media for the democratic process by referring to the different dimensions that constitute citizenship. He identifies three important ways in which the communication media contribute to the constitution of citizenship. First, in order for people to be able to exercise their full rights as citizens, they must have access to information about their rights. They will need advice on, and analysis of how they can pursue these rights effectively. Secondly, the citizens must have access to the broadest possible range of information, interpretation and debate on areas that involve public political choices. They must be able to use different kinds of media to register and express criticism, and come forward with alternative models for development. They should be able to do this on the basis of information on and interpretation of events locally, nationally and internationally. Thirdly, people must be able to recognise themselves and their aspirations, their cultures and life styles, in the range of representations offered by various media, and they should be able to contribute to developing and extending these representations. Media, therefore, are linked to identity formation, particularly of a collective kind, and may be seen as interacting with various social movements. These often develop their own media, often as an alternative to the mainstream media. Thus, the interaction between expressions of various identities and positions in various media forms are ideally part of the process of creating a democratic public sphere.

An important function identified here, which is found in almost all of the literature on the role of media in relation to democratic processes, is the significance of information and the presentation of alternative viewpoints. The media should inform citizens on matters of public policy by presenting and debating alternatives. This has to do with the concept of rights that citizens have as members of a society. The media can contribute to empowering their readers, listeners and viewers by making them aware of their civil and political rights, and of why and how these rights should be exercised. *People who do not know their rights, have no way of exercising their rights.* On the basis of this, there exists a preconception about media and human rights, and media and the principle of freedom of expression. This again is linked to a fundamental perception of the relationship between democratic processes and egalitarianism, and here the agenda of market liberalism, with a concept of a strict division between State and society, parts ways with a more social- and rights-oriented interpretation of the role of communication systems and democracy. In a democracy, audiences should be treated as both consumers and citizens, and constitute a public.

The second category of roles identified by Murdock includes the watchdog role of the media in uncovering and publicising political corruption, other abuses of power, and inept policies. Ideally, this should lead to public concern and citizens' furore, which should impel reform in official behaviour. In other words, the media should, by being dedicated to providing information, alternative debate and criticism, contribute to more effective, transparent and accountable governance.

The third aspect of Murdock's criteria has less to do with the media as information agent and centres for debate, and more to do with their entertainment and cultural functions, and thus with the relationship between media and forms of identities. To fulfil these ideals, a media system needs to be multifaceted, open, and cater for a variety of interests, both social and cultural. Centrally placed and marginalised groups must be allowed a voice. It is important to remember that media appeal to reason and to emotions, and this may create problems particularly in situations where identities are expressed as fundamental and oppose other identities.

Lastly, freedom of speech is a fundamental value of the democratic process and should be protected against government interference. The damage involved in restricting freedom of expression is so great that even proven harm resulting from free speech should not be prohibited unless it is of a severe degree. Many will argue that not only harm, but also offence, can constitute grounds for restricting the freedom of expression. However, as offence is intrinsically tied to morality, offence cannot constitute sufficient grounds for censorship. A democratic state has no business in legislating morality. Indeed, deeply held beliefs and moral convictions often need to be challenged. A culture that legislates against offence is one that not only fails to protect the basic freedoms of individuals, but also one likely to stagnate and infantilise its citizens.

To summarise the ideal functions of the media:

- The media should give a truthful, comprehensive and insightful account of events, locally and internationally, in a context that gives them meaning.
- The media should provide a forum for the exchange of comments and criticisms.
- The media should project a representative picture of the constituent groups in the society.
- The media should present and clarify the goals and values of society.
- The media should provide full access to information and knowledge, for citizens to make sense of their situation.
- Freedom of expression should be recognised, and the media should not in any way be censored.

How is the situation in southern Africa seen in relation to a principled view of the role of the media in the democratic process? What are the constraints? And how can the media's role be analysed on the basis of principled, if not universal, democratic ideals? It is important to be aware of the substantial differences between the experiences of the countries of the SADC region, ranging from apartheid South Africa to war-ravaged and poverty-stricken Angola and Mozambique. However, there may be some common experiences providing the background for some general conclusions. One of the most interesting aspects is how the media, in a way reminiscent of what Benedict Anderson[14] analyses as 'the rise of print-capitalism', particularly in post-apartheid South Africa, may have contributed to the formation of a new form of national cohesion, not imposed, but formed in the public arena. In the distinct historical situations referred to above and below, the processes have involved the defence of fragile democratic institutions and the establishment and re-establishment of democratic practices. The role of the media in general has been to sustain democratic 'discourses' and contribute to the agenda for the development of the democratic project, and to serve as a critical voice in relation to authoritarian governments.

In cases where, for various reasons, the political parties or organisations failed to provide an effective opposition to the ruling party, whether through fragmentation or inexperience, the opposition originated partly from the media, not least through its watchdog function by exposing abuse of power and corruption. For example, in Zimbabwe, until 2000, an organised political opposition was virtually non-existent in what may be characterised as a de facto one-party state. The independent press, in the form of weeklies and monthly magazines have, however, contributed significantly to the democratic process by voicing alternative viewpoints, representing interests different from the ruling party's, questioning the policy of the government and exposing abuse of power and corruption. The independent press and active trade unions and organisations of civil society have, in conjunction with an independent judiciary, kept Zimbabwean society relatively open.

Even if democratic change has taken place, the experiences of new democracies in many parts of the world indicate that fears about lingering authoritarianism are not unfounded. In the realm of the media, this is particularly pronounced in relation to the broadcast media. Governments are often reluctant to yield control over broadcasting, or to permit alternative radio and television stations. A case in point is that of Zimbabwe. The relationship between the State and the media is central to the discussion of media and democracy. There seems to be mutual antagonism between governments, both newly elected and old ones, and the independent press.

Many ministers, officials and even presidents condemn the press for what they perceive as misrepresentation, irresponsible reporting, sensationalism, and outright lies. The accusations from government sources tend to centre on reports about government activities, and there are often veiled threats in the attacks; sometimes the threats are even put into practice. The relationship between the press and government should ideally be one of critical distance, but not necessarily one of hostility. Currently, it appears that, in many African countries, there is a situation where the so-called 'official' media maintain a too close and uncritical relationship with government, while the independent press often has a tendency for sensationalism and rumour mongering.

THE CHALLENGE OF COMMUNICATION
DEVELOPMENTS

Throughout the world, the media are gaining in importance, and the relationship between the media and society consequently becomes problematic.[15] Firstly, the media are widely believed to have gained in their centrality and potential influence for good or ill in society. Secondly, the media undergo rapid change, mainly because of new technology, with the consequence that existing frameworks of regulation and social control are becoming obsolete. The principal dilemma is how to reconcile the increasing significance of media with the declining capacity for control on behalf of the general good. This applies especially to television, which in many parts of the world, though not in Africa, is the dominant medium for public communication. Historically, it is also the medium that has been most subject to regulation.

The loss of control stems in part from the increasing difficulty of effective supervision of new electronic media and of the ever-multiplying number of television channels, both satellite and cable. Other factors of the time also play their role. One factor is the greatly increased economic imperative to harness market forces to communication development, moving towards the widely shared goal of the information society. The pace and direction of media development are increasingly determined by powerful global corporations rather than by governments, as was the case not so long ago. The triumph of liberal ideology, and the spirit of deregulation and privatisation, makes it harder than ever for societies to intervene and exert control.

The implied dispute between political and economic interests is made more complex by the need to protect rights to free expression. This in itself has brought into question many of the controls traditionally applied to broadcasting. The media have never been happy with restrictions on their freedom of action, in whatever form, although economic motives for opposition are often hard to disentangle from principled resistance. Media in the form of powerful transnational corporations have more scope for resisting unwanted interference or checks from national governments. The combined effect of the forces at work is to weaken the political capacity and the will to set restraints on the media on behalf of the general good of society, even if the means should be available.

The very notion of what counts as the general good of society is itself less clear-cut than it used to be in the days when national elites largely decided what it was and applied their criteria to media systems within national frontiers. The transnationalisation of media is a potent source of uncertainty, since individuals can claim wider allegiances, and flows of public communication are no longer determined by national governments alone.

On a global stage, the goals of a more balanced flow of communication, a more equitable access to information and cultural goods, and a more ethical treatment of world problems, seem to be receding. Everywhere, answers are being sought as to the best way to develop new electronic media and how to integrate it into existing systems of regulation, in order to protect and advance the fundamental interests of society.

The economic marginalisation of Africa, with a significant part of the population living on the margins of a real market, creates three problems. The first is that the true international market media become strong in relation to the tastes of the minority economic elite, overshadowing their interests and identification with national, possibly more pluralistic and immediately relevant media and issues.[16] Secondly, the information and media gap between the information-strong and information-weak parts of the world are not going to disappear, despite the over-optimistic pronouncements that the Internet will usher in a new era of democratic communication. It is important to remind ourselves of some basic facts. Tokyo, with a population of 23 million, has three times as many working telephone lines as the whole of the Africa, with its population of 580 million. Only one person in ten in the world has ever made a telephone call. One per cent of the earth's population has access to the Internet, and the vast majority live in the northern hemisphere. And, most serious of all, only one third of the world's population can afford to buy a book – the oldest and still maybe the most important of media.[17] Thirdly, because of the uneven development and bifurcation of African societies, the rural population will have access only to a very limited variety of media. This, linked to the likelihood of increased contradictions between elites and the masses, may threaten the common identity of belonging to a greater community of citizens, and prompt the falling back on primary identities.

ETHICAL AND LEGAL FRAMEWORKS

Laws play a central role in framing some of the most important problems related to media ethics, in the context of the freedom of the press and the right to free expression, and the right to access information. Laws also play a role in how the media may deal with issues such as privacy and telling the truth. Laws regulating the media may, of course, be discussed as a form of infringement on the freedom of the press.

THE RIGHT TO KNOW AND ACCESS TO INFORMATION

One of the extensions of the principle of freedom of expression is 'the right to know'. The argument is that free speech will be without value if the public cannot obtain the information it needs, from government and other bodies, to be able to discuss important issues. Without going too deeply into the many philosophical and theoretical problems raised by this issue, it should be possible to define areas of information about which the public has a right to know. The most important of these pertains to what government is doing because this affects the public as citizens. Similarly, the activities of nongovernmental organisations and, occasionally, private companies, affect the public. Where the public has an interest, the press has a mandate to inform. The public has a legitimate interest in all information about matters that might affect the welfare of society. The claim, then, is for freedom of information. Some countries have Freedom of Information Acts; others do not.

Several countries, particularly in Europe, provide a clear constitutional right of citizens' access to information held by the government. The principle is that all documents are public unless a statute expressly permits exceptions. Even when a request appears to touch on one of the excepted areas, the authorities must weigh the interest in disclosure against the interest in secrecy. The law often favours citizens' rights by, for example, compelling governments to deal with requests within a day or to provide reasons for the delay. This constitutional right of access is often implied in the provisions that guarantee freedom of expression and press freedom. Government authorities are only entitled to withhold information that could affect national security or defence. In most countries, information is also exempt if disclosure would impair international relations, law enforcement, public safety, personal privacy or commercial secrecy.

Even if countries constitutionally secure freedom of access to most government documents, in practice, the authorities of very liberal countries have been known to withhold information that could embarrass them. In such cases, journalists often tend not to be too vigorous in their pursuit of government-held information. But it should be the duty of journalists to pursue the matter in the interest of the public's right to know and to ensure full transparency in the way public policy is being conducted.

Refusal of information is, in most countries that provide for freedom of access, subject to administrative review either by a body specifically constituted to oversee compliance with the disclosure laws, or by a general administrative body. Decisions made by these bodies may be appealed through the courts. The availability of administrative review by a specially constituted body is useful in that it can facilitate speedier attention to complaints, although administrative delay is a problem that plagues even the most open of countries.

Austria, Sweden and the USA offer strong protection to the press for publishing government secrets. In Austria and Sweden, journalists and editors are not subject to prosecution for publishing official secrets, unless the disclosure risks severe damage to national defence or international relations. Moreover, in Sweden, journalists cannot be compelled to reveal the source of a government leak unless disclosure severely endangers national security. In turn, the journalist's right to refuse provides considerable protection for public sector employees who 'blow the whistle' on government misconduct. In the USA, the press may not be prosecuted for publishing virtually any secret information; the only publication that will subject the press to liability is when the names of intelligence agents are disclosed, when there is a pattern of such publication and when publication is likely to impair intelligence activities. In several countries, the fact that disclosure serves the public interest is a defence for the publication of information collected by illegal means, and for any government employee who leaked information.

However, even in countries that do not punish the press for publishing information, any civil servant who leaks information is generally liable for breach of confidentiality and may be subject to criminal or civil liability or dismissal. In some countries there is no law establishing a duty of confidentiality to the government. And in others, such as France, the UK and Canada, it is a crime to publish secret defence information, and there is no public interest defence for the press or the employee who supplied the information. Generally, in southern Africa, access to government information is restricted, the Official Secrets Acts are strict, and the law is weighed against the press for publishing such information.

When it comes to access to and disclosure of court documents and proceedings, the principle of open trials is respected in most European countries, and receives constitutional protection. However, there exist certain exceptions, either in law or in practice. Most countries permit trials, or parts of trials, to be closed in order to protect the rights of the litigants (and, especially, to protect the fair trial rights of criminal defendants), fundamental privacy interests of the witnesses, national security interests, and/or the interests of juveniles. In some countries, trials involving family matters and children are presumptively closed. Several countries have special rules regarding rape cases, including the exclusion of the public at the request of the victim and bans on the publication of the victim's name or identifying characteristics. Similarly, cases involving mental patients, guardianship and adoption proceedings are often private.

The courts in several countries tend to favour openness, and will not punish publication of confidential court information (unless the information was secret for independent reasons). Where a judge rather than a jury tries cases, concerns about prejudging guilt and impairing fair trial rights generally are greatly reduced. Pre-trial proceedings, unlike trials, are closed in many civil law countries. In the common law countries, to which most southern African countries belong, the presumption of openness extends to pre-trial proceedings, although it is not as strong as the presumption of trial openness. In the USA, most pre-trial proceedings are open, and the press may publish anything disclosed in open court or forms part of the public record. In contrast, in the UK it is a contempt of court to publish any information or opinions that create a substantial risk of prejudice to the course of justice while a case is *sub judice* or 'active' (in a criminal case, from the moment a suspect has been charged or arrested until the decision of any appeal). The risk of prejudice is deemed greatest in criminal trials by jury, and least in cases tried by a professional judge or on appeal. After the events of 11 September 2001, with the terrorist attacks in New York and Washington DC, several countries, including the USA, have proposed special terrorist laws that severely limit the rights of the accused and the possibility of public scrutiny of court procedures. Such laws are highly questionable in light of the principle of judicial openness, and basic human and democratic rights.

... access to and disclosure of legislative documents and proceedings should be regarded as an important part of the democratic process.

The principle of access to and disclosure of legislative documents and proceedings should be regarded as an important part of the democratic process. Consequently, parliamentary sessions are generally public in democratic countries, and in some countries, openness is mandated by the constitution. Exceptions are permitted in certain circumstances, such as when classified information is to be discussed. There may also be a presumption of access to sessions of parliamentary committees. In several countries, parliamentary committees are presumptively closed and neither the press nor the public may have access to their proceedings or documents. However, in most countries, there is no penalty for disclosure by the press of committee or other non-public documents, unless the documents were entitled to secrecy for some other substantive reason. In most countries, all statements made during a parliamentary session are absolutely privileged (that is, they cannot form the basis of an offence), as is good faith reporting about statements made during public sessions.

In the common law jurisdictions of the UK, the USA, Canada and Australia, a person may be held in contempt of parliament (or congress), and fined or imprisoned, for directly or indirectly impeding parliament in performing its functions, such as by (in the UK) bringing parliaments or legislative assemblies into contempt or ridicule, or contribute to diminishing respect for parliament. Such laws may, if used in Draconian manner, limit the possibilities for political satire, and the laws are now, in general, not enforced. Even in the UK, no one has been imprisoned this century. In the USA, the contempt power, which has been used only to punish the refusal to provide requested evidence, has rarely been exercised against the press. However, laws such as the above have, on occasion, been used to threaten the press and oppositional politicians in some African countries.

While there is a general tendency towards opening government and official documents to public scrutiny, issues regarding commercial secrecy and access to information held by private persons is much more complex. In several countries, employees are obliged by statute or common law not to disclose the business secrets of their employers. In some, however, this obligation does not prevent the disclosure of information about illegal actions or other wrongdoing. In such instances, the freedoms of expression and information must be balanced against an employee's duty of confidentiality, and will outweigh any duty of loyalty as far as matters of public importance are concerned.

In some countries, even though employees may be punished for disclosure, the press may not be prosecuted for publication.

Most countries do not protect employees who disclose information about their employer's wrongdoing from termination of contracts or other disciplinary measures, even if their disclosures were in the public interest and/or were not unlawful. There is a contrast between the open access approach to government information and the protection of public sector 'whistle-blowers' and a markedly restrictive approach to information held by the private sector.

In some countries, private whistle-blowers are protected by the constitution to the extent that journalists may not divulge their identity if given information in confidence. However, there is no legislation discouraging employers from conducting investigations and disciplining those they find to be 'leaks'. In some countries, even though employees may be punished for disclosure, the press may not be prosecuted for publication.

Increasingly, companies are required to make public information relevant to environmental protection. For example, companies are required to supply considerable information about waste disposal to the government, and such information is generally available to the public. Alternatively, citizens have the right to access to some environmental information on, for example, hazardous substances, pollution and waste disposal, from local government authorities.

Subversity and official secrets

One of the most sinister aspects of the legal regulations pertaining to the relationship between government and the media is found in Official Secrets Acts, which exist throughout the world, but can vary radically in their scope. The primary purpose of such legislation is to protect the secrets of the State, which include defence and economic interests, and to prevent terrorist activities. It is essential for national security that defence installations are protected against spies who might use the information, maps or drawings to help foreign enemies in the event of war or attack. Any leaked defence information might jeopardise the war efforts of the country. To a certain extent, military operations must be protected by law against espionage and from the disclosure of military secrets and military installations. It is also essential to prevent the circulation of certain government documents that are sensitive or still under discussion, and which may include information about the conduct of foreign affairs. Governments can also withhold information that is pending – for example, information on scientific research, intelligence activities and criminal investigations. It is apparent, therefore, that Official Secrets Acts may have a legitimate role in protecting State interests.

It is also important for the principles of freedom of expression and information that the limitations to such laws are stringent, and that they are not used to prevent the public from having access to information relevant to the public debate about the state of the nation. It is important to ensure, however, that these laws are not being used to protect government and public officials against the exposure of abuse of power. The majority of such acts in southern African are inheritances from the colonial period, and much legal and press opinion holds that they give government too far-reaching powers and thus contravene democratic principles. Such legislation may breed a culture of secrecy and result in public opinion based on inadequate information.

In order to illustrate the role of this form of legislation, we will look at the situation in Zimbabwe.[17] The Constitution of Zimbabwe protects freedom of expression, but this is deemed to exist only when it does not impinge on other interests, such as State interests.

The Constitution states that it is not unconstitutional to have laws made to protect public and private interests, providing the law is reasonably justified in a democracy. There are no provisions for right to access to information in the Constitution, and public officials have no legal obligation to supply the media with information when requested to do so. Instead, there are laws that permit public officials to decline to give information to the media. The Official Secrets Act of 1970:

> ... prohibits the disclosure, for any purpose prejudicial to the safety or interests of Zimbabwe, of information which might be useful to an enemy; to make provision for the purpose of preventing persons from obtaining or disclosing official secrets ... prevent trespass upon defence works, fortifications, military reserves and other prohibited places.

Sections 4(1), 5(1), 5(2) and 8 set out the prohibitions and offences related to journalistic performance. These provisions seek to regulate the publication, possession and retention of information:

> Any person who has in his possession or under his control any secret official code or password or any model, article, document or information which
>
> (a) relates to or is used in a prohibited place or relates to anything in a prohibited place; or
>
> (b) has been made or obtained in contravention of the provisions of this Act; or
>
> (c) has been entrusted in confidence to him by a person holding an office in the service of the State; or
>
> (d) he has obtained or to which he has had access owing to his position as a person who holds or has held office in the service of the State, or as a person who holds or has held a contract made on behalf of the State, or a contract, the performance of which in whole or in part is carried out in a prohibited place, or as a person who is or has been employed under a person who holds or has held such an office or contract; and who
>
> (e) communicates such code, password, model, article, document or information to any person, other than a person to whom he is authorised to communicate it, is liable to prosecution.

The Act makes it an offence to communicate to the media any information, no matter how trivial it may be, or even if that information has no effect on national security or public order. The scope of the Act is such that journalists have the dilemma of determining whether or not the information they have is covered by the Act. It is tempting to government departments to use the Official Secrets Act to prevent the publication of information merely because its disclosure would be embarrassing. As the legislation stands, all government information is included, no matter how trivial.

The Act is a relic from the authoritarian colonial regime. It was promulgated in a war situation to deal primarily with internal security problems. The legislation was used to suppress information about the atrocities committed by the Rhodesian forces on rural people, and to counteract pressure from the international community, which had imposed sanctions. The legislation was also intended to suppress opposition from white liberals supporting calls for independence. The Act was therefore never meant to deal with what can normally be called 'official secrets'. It resulted from a desperate effort by an authoritarian regime to prolong its unjust and repressive rule, and to shield itself from its enemies; it controlled information that was unfavourable to the regime.

The continued existence of the Official Secrets Act in Zimbabwe has had a negative impact on the flow of information from government departments to the media. As the Act stands, government officials cannot pass information to the media without authorisation. And the media cannot go directly to the government departments to get information, unless they have been invited to a press conference or through press releases. The procedure is that, when the media need information from specific departments, questions must be put in writing to the Ministry of Information, which, in turn, forwards them to the department/s concerned. It does not matter whether the information sought is of little significance. According to journalists, this bureaucratic procedure takes so long that, by the time information is obtained, it is outdated. Because access to information is limited, journalists often resort to rumours, speculation or information from unauthorised sources within government departments, risking prosecution.

An example that illustrates how the Act contravenes important democratic principles is a case from 1993. Basildon Peta, a journalist working for an independent newspaper, *The Daily Gazette* (which ceased publication in December 1994) received confidential documents from a civil servant working in the tax department, which showed that some companies part-owned by the ruling ZANU(PF) and the government-related newspaper company, Zimbabwe Newspapers (1980) Ltd were evading tax. The type of information was embarrassing to the government, which frequently blamed private companies for not paying taxes.

Following the publication of the story, Peta was detained, interrogated and harassed by secret agents who wanted to know his source of information. Both he and the editor, Brian Latham, were charged with contravening the Act. The charges were later dropped, although no reason was stated. Peta claims that the secret agents were primarily concerned about the source of information rather than the truth of the story. After the incident, no mention was made of whether investigations were opened to verify the allegation that some companies were not paying tax.

The Peta case brings into question when the Official Secrets Act should be used. According to the existing Act, the information Peta had obtained was classified as a government secret and, accordingly, he should have been charged for contravening the law. The government apparently dropped the case because it knew that revelations in court would have been more damaging. If Peta had not been brave enough to withhold the name of his source, that source could have been victimised. If the source had not given Peta the information, the public would not have known about the corrupt practices in the tax department. The Peta case was an attempt by government to intimidate journalists and to prevent them from publishing unauthorised information. It is apparent that the legislation insulates government departments from public scrutiny.

Another case that illustrates conflicts between what the press sees as legitimate public concerns over policies conducted by the government comes from Zambia. In March 1999, the editor and eight journalists from the independent newspaper *The Post* were arrested for espionage. Paramilitary police also sealed *The Post* editorial offices and halted the printing of an edition. All editorial and printing staff found working were locked up for two days.

The background to the case was an article that was published in *The Post* titled 'Angola Worries Zambia Army, ZAF', which contained unconfirmed details of Zambia's alleged military deficiencies compared to Angola with which Lusaka was engaged in a war of words over alleged supply of arms to the rebel UNITA movement. *The Post*, quoting unnamed senior army and air force officers, claimed that Zambia could not withstand a military attack by Angola because, comparatively, the Angolan army was far superior in terms of strength, training and experience.

The report disclosed in detail the military equipment the Zambian army is alleged to possess, its fighting units and number of tanks. The reasons for disclosing such information were complex, but they involved at least two principled arguments. The first was that it was in the interest of the Zambian population to know about the state of the defence forces in the country and that to debate defence policies on the basis of thorough knowledge was a legitimate public concern. The second argument was linked to the accusation of Zambia supplying arms to UNITA, and that to have all the facts in relation to this in the open was legitimate public concern as it involved political principles of how the country should conduct its foreign policy. Thirdly the editor of *The Post* maintained that, as editor-in-chief, he was responsible for the story, not the journalists, and that the government used the story to arrest staff of the newspaper so that the article would be prevented from appearing, and that the action thus was an attack on the freedom of the press.

Zambian authorities claimed that the article compromised the country's security by exposing military secrets 'to the enemy', and charged the editor and the journalists with espionage. The points of view of the government in this case were clearly reflected in an editorial in the official newspaper *The Times of Zambia* (10 March 1999), which stated:

> *The Post* newspaper without any doubt has breached and overstepped its limits.
>
> Plainly and simply, by displaying in detail the state of Zambia's defence arsenal, the newspaper has undressed the republic before the region, let alone the world at large, to borrow an expression used in Parliament by Mr Christopher Chawinga. Pressmen and women do not function in their own world, an insulated territory in which their deeds are unquestionable and in which they are their own law. They function in a world in which their desires and interests must be balanced against the hopes and aspirations of others.
>
> The point is that press freedom is not absolute and boundless. Media professionals and their organisations do not have the absolute right to publish and be damned. Rather, they bear on their shoulders the responsibility to aid and preserve, not dismantle, society. Because society should be preserved and not dismantled, there are laws against exposing Zambia's defence capacity anyhow – even to citizens themselves. To expose a nation's defence resource as *The Post* has done is to aid the enemy, and therefore to dismantle and disgrace the nation.

Every nation has its security to protect. National security everywhere on earth is sacrosanct. Even in the developed world, this is so strongly upheld that in war situations, military censors must clear news material before it is made public. It happens because a journalist may consider crucially newsworthy a certain discovery or development which if published may actually equip and forearm enemy forces.

[...]

Our Head of State has to be commended for enduring floods of personal offence, injury and insult all in the interest of building our young democracy, which includes freedom of press and of speech. In other countries within the region, newspapers like *The Post* would have closed years ago.

Censorship in times of war, or threat of war, is international practice even in advanced democracies. A careless comment or report could easily throw a country into flames.

However, *The Post* has reported not carelessly but diligently, studiously and deliberately. It looks like the editors simply decided to dare Government and see what would happen. That behaviour is simply outside the perimeters of journalism and nobody should sympathise with newsmen and women who themselves do not care about endangering their own country.

Media access to information held by government is a prerequisite to democracy. If the government is unchecked, unfairness, abuse of power, inefficiency, corruption and lack of concern for human rights may prevail. Such vices normally thrive in secretive environments. In a democracy, the media should strive to make sure that most government functions remain open for inspection. This role is curtailed by the Official Secrets legislation that has been used – not only to protect legitimate government secrets, but also to cover up blunders and corruption by government officials, and to prevent public access to arguments in a free and open debate about crucial issues for the future of society. In both the Zimbabwean and the Zambian cases referred to above, there are indications that Official Secrets legislation is being used to prevent public insight and debate.

Law and Order (Maintenance) Acts

Press freedom may also be limited by Law and Order (Maintenance) Acts. In this context, we shall use the Zimbabwean Act and its application to illustrate the principles involved. The Act protects the interests of defence, public security and maintenance of law, subversive statements, prevention of alarm or despondency, or statements likely to disturb public peace. The provisions of the Act dealing with these are Sections 44 and 49. Section 44 prohibits the publication of a subversive statement by the press. A subversive statement includes a statement that is likely:

i)   to bring the President in person into hatred or contempt;

ii)   to excite disaffection against the President in person or the Government or Constitution

iii) to incite any person to commit a crime in disturbance of the public peace;

iv)   to engender or promote feelings of hostility to, or expose to contempt, ridicule or disesteem any group, section or class in a community

v)   to induce any person to resist, either actively or passively, any law or lawful administrative measure.

A person who utters, distributes, writes or displays a subversive statement is liable to imprisonment for a period not exceeding five years. A person can defend himself/herself against prosecution only if he or she can satisfy the court that the subversive statement was made in good faith and with the intention:

a)   of showing that the President or the Government has been misled or mistaken in any measure;

b)   of pointing out errors or defects in the Government or Constitution;

c)   of urging any person to attempt to procure by lawful means the alteration of any matter in Zimbabwe established by law.

Section 49 prohibits the publication of false statements. It is a serious offence to make, publish or reproduce a statement that is likely to cause fear, alarm or despondency among the public or any section of the public, or which is likely to disturb the public peace. Anyone found guilty of contravening this section is liable to a prison sentence not exceeding seven years unless he or she can satisfy the court that reasonable steps were taken to verify the accuracy of the statement.

The Law and Order (Maintenance) Act was enacted on 2 December 1960 by the Rhodesian regime. On its enactment, white liberals, church leaders and African nationalists vehemently opposed it. Throughout the colonial era, the Act was used to deal with opponents of the regime. Criticism of the Smith regime, no matter how genuine, amounted to subversion. Several African nationalists were prosecuted for allegedly making subversive statements when, in fact, they were genuinely opposed to the repressive nature of the Rhodesian government towards the black majority. These nationalists included the current president, Robert Mugabe, who was prosecuted for telling black people in Highfield, a residential suburb of Harare, that they were imprisoned for demanding land. Former Vice President Joshua Nkomo and the later Speaker of Parliament, Didymus Mutasa, were also prosecuted for criticising the regime's policies towards black Zimbabweans. The Smith regime did not tolerate any criticism from black nationalists, churches and white liberals. Critical church publications like *Moto* were banned for criticising the regime, as were newspapers sympathetic to black people, like *The Daily News*, *Chapupu* and the *Zimbabwe Sun*. Ironically, the same nationalists who had suffered the brunt of the Act left it intact when they ascended to government on independence. Some even defended it. When Justice Minister Emmerson Mnangagwa was asked when the Act would be repealed by delegates at a Human Rights Conference held in Harare in September 1992, he invited delegates to come to his office and point out the provisions of the Act that they felt infringed human rights. In 1993, he reiterated that there was nothing wrong with the Act at a Press Freedom conference in Kadoma. In 1996, Home Affairs Minister Dumiso Dabengwa defended police brutality on a peaceful demonstration by civil servants, by citing that their actions were justified under the Law and Order (Maintenance) Act.

This brief historical background reveals that the Act is a violation of the Universal Declaration of Human Rights and, arguably, violates the Constitution of Zimbabwe. It goes far beyond what is expected of a democracy. It can be argued that the Act is very wide in its scope of what constitutes a subversive statement and public order. There is no proper limit to what statements can be deemed subversive and, as such, the Act can be improperly used. Publications that reveal corruption by the president or government can be interpreted as subversive. Journalists are thus constrained by the problem of drawing a line between criticism that constitutes subversion and criticism that does not. The law gives the government opportunity for intolerance of criticism, and thus provides it with an undemocratic tool for stifling opposition. If, without foundation, criticism imputes corrupt motives to certain politicians, the remedy should be through civil defamation laws. The argument is that there is no justification for public officials to resort to prosecuting 'subversion' when they are criticised. In a democracy, public officials are expected to be tolerant of criticism from the public and the media, which should be on guard against the abuse of powers by office bearers. Law should not be composed in such a way as to curtail the role of the media in criticising those in government. The Act does not balance the competing interests and it does not have adequate checks against abuse. The only check upon the exercise of these powers (if, indeed, it can be called a check), is that, before a Minister takes action to prohibit publications, he or she is obliged to refer the matter to a committee of persons appointed by the Minister for confirmation that the publications would be likely to have the aforesaid effects. The Act is restrictive in that there is little defence available for the media to appeal against subversive statements. It is also restrictive in that any statement considered subversive may attract a sentence of up to five years in terms of Section 44 and up to seven years in terms of Section 49. This alone, is enough to make journalists cautious about whom they cover and what they write about. The imprisonment of journalists for media offences is an impediment to press freedom.

In a democracy, public officials are expected to be tolerant of criticism from the public and the media ...

The Act has been applied or used as a threat several times, among others early in 1999 to two newspaper stories relating to the presence of Zimbabwean troops in the civil war in the Democratic Republic of Congo (DRC), where Zimbabwe supported the government troops of President Laurent Kabila. It started when the independent Sunday newspaper *The Zimbabwe Standard* (10 January 1999) claimed that there had been an attempted military coup and that 23 officers had been arrested. The newspaper reported that the plans for the coup were based on widespread dissatisfaction in the army and in Zimbabwean society with the country's involvement in the civil war in the DRC. Some days after the publication of the story, military police stormed the offices of the *Standard*, and subsequently arrested the editor, Mark Chavunduka, and reporter, Raymond Choto, who had written the story. Chavunduka and Choto alleged, and medical reports indicated, that they were severely tortured during the nine days they were held in military detention. During the torture and interrogation, the military police wanted to know who their military sources were and especially the alleged link with South African military intelligence. The military police also wanted to know the source of funding of the newspapers, and threatened to arrest other senior people in the Independent Newspapers company, as well as the people working for another independent weekly *The Zimbabwe Mirror*.

The two journalists were only transferred to the civil police and formally charged after a judge had ruled that their arrest was unconstitutional, and that they should be released. This did not take place until some days later, and after the Minister of Defence, Moven Mahachi, had been threatened with contempt of court charges, because he had stated that his ministry did not take orders from courts. When they appeared in court, the journalists were charged under the Law and Order (Maintenance) Act for the publication of 'false news' and 'spreading alarm and despondency'. The State alleged that the story had not been verified and was meant to tarnish the image of the Zimbabwe Defence Forces and cause public disorder. However, Chavunduka and Choto, in their statements to the police, denied that their story was bound to cause 'alarm, despondency and public disorder' since the alleged coup had been quelled. They also said that they had taken reasonable steps to verify the story with the Defence ministry, but without success. Two days later, the newspaper's publisher, Clive Wilson, was also arrested, but released after a weekend in custody without being charged.

Whatever the true version of the coup story, the events are yet another example of the conflict between the Zimbabwean government and the independent media. This was also clearly borne out in the statements made by government about the events: Minister Mahachi said, among other things, that the independent media had a well-calculated programme to destroy the country and the ZANU(PF) government. He said that, while the government fully recognised the freedom of the press, as enshrined in the Constitution of Zimbabwe, it also had the responsibility to protect the nation from malicious misinformation deliberately intended to create instability by some newspapers because of financial greed, and that the independent press had a hidden agenda. Chen Chimutengwende, the then Minister of Information, said that he wished that Chavunduka could stay in detention for good, because his newspaper was full of lies, and that the independent media were out to sabotage and destabilise Zimbabwe, and that this was tantamount to treason. Events, particularly after the elections in 2000, and further grave attacks on the independent press, have shown that the arrests in January 1999, and the government attacks on the independent press then, was but the beginning of something more serious to come.

The struggle between the government and the independent press in Zimbabwe over how to interpret the crisis-ridden situation in the country, particularly in relation to its heavy engagement in the civil war in the DRC, did not end with this. Three weeks later, the editor and three journalists from *The Zimbabwe Mirror* were arrested for having written about the dissatisfaction within the army over their military engagement in the DRC. The editor-in-chief, Ibbo Mandaza, and the journalist behind the story, Grace Kwinjeh, were both charged with 'publishing false information likely to cause alarm, fear and despondency'.[19] A particularly interesting aspect of this latest arrest is that Ibbo Mandaza is not typical of Zimbabwean editors, and he does not share the same political background as the owners and journalists of the Independent group. His background is in ZANU(PF), in exile during the war, and he served in senior civil servant and political positions during the 1980s. He is primarily an intellectual and a high-profile social scientist, who initiated the setting up of one of the most important independent social science research institutions in Africa, The SAPES Trust. His critical position in relation to government policy, and principled defence of democratic principles, may be seen as indicative of the widening split in the party over the role of the leadership's increasingly dictatorial policies.

The government's perspective on this confrontation with the press was summed up in the following excerpt from a letter in the Johannesburg newspaper *The Star* (19 March 1999) from the Zimbabwean High Commissioner to South Africa:

> The fact of the matter is that the arrest of the journalists followed persistent, false and malicious reports aimed at destabilising the army. Some of the stories included the following:
>
> - That a soldier died in battle in the Democratic Republic of Congo and only his head was brought home for burial;
> - That there was mutiny by soldiers in the DRC;
> - That 23 officers in the Zimbabwe National Army had been arrested for planning a coup.
>
> On the first allegation, the soldier in question died of malaria while on duty in the DRC and his body had to be exhumed in order to prove that the story was without foundation. That there was mutiny by the Zimbabwe Army in the DRC proved to be a complete fabrication as the soldiers continue to serve with the unquestionable loyalty expected of a disciplined and well-trained army.
>
> The coup plot story was without foundation, and yet it cost the country's image abroad dearly.

Regarding the alleged torture of journalists, we wish to state that the Zimbabwe Government does not condone the use of torture. It is for this reason that this matter is being taken up with the courts. The logical thing for the press in general therefore is for it to be patient enough to wait for the law to take its course instead of rushing to unsubstantiated conclusions.

While the facts of the cases may be disputable, the legal apparatus used by government in its struggle to control which issues are to be debated, confirm what the independent media and human rights organisations in Zimbabwe have alleged since the early 1990s – that the government treats all non-official media like an opposition party, and as enemies of the State. It is a conflict that illustrates how a power-conscious and increasingly corrupt authoritarian government feels threatened by open media, particularly over issues that involve struggle within the governing party. It also illustrates how problematic Law and Order (Maintenance) Acts are to the furthering of public debate, and how they may be used to force the independent media not to be critical of government. Thus, the existence of such laws and the threat to use them instils an atmosphere of fear in the media, and may lead to a widespread practice of self-censorship. Such acts, there-fore, are at the centre of a fundamental question of media ethics.

DEFAMATION

Defamation is one of the most problematic areas both in relation to media law and to the relationship between the media and the public, the media and official and private secrecies, and opportunities for the press to conduct investigative journalism. In several countries, heavy penalties and strict defamation laws effectively curb an open press and opportunities for the public to gain access to shady deals and abuses of power involving, for example, corruption. While defamation and libel are, strictly speaking, part of the legal system, they are also central to the role of democratic media and to issues in media ethics.

The main issue seems to be the contradiction between the right to personal reputation, which is constitutionally protected in many coun-tries, and the fundamental importance of the rights of the press to impart, and of the public to receive, information and opinions. Most countries provide statutory protection for the right to reputation and/or personal honour, and defamation may be both a criminal offence and a civil tort. In some countries where criminal actions previously were more common, there has been a trend towards greater use of civil law.

In others, civil actions have for a long time been more common. In the USA, criminal defamation laws lapsed into disuse by the 1950s (and would today be found unconstitutional unless limited to statements that were likely to cause an imminent breach of the peace). In the UK, criminal libel remains part of the common law, although virtually unused in recent years. In France, Germany and Sweden, civil and criminal actions may take place before the same court at the same time. If convicted, a defendant may be ordered to pay a criminal fine to the State in addition to civil damages to the injured party.

In several countries, truth is a complete defence for defamation based on an allegation of fact. In others, the plaintiff bears the burden of proving that damaging facts were untrue, or proving the statement's falsity, at least when it relates to a matter of public concern. In the UK and many other common law countries, truth is not a defence, although public interest may be. The drawback of requiring the press to prove truth is that responsible journalists often rely on sources who insist on remaining anonymous, thus making proof virtually impossible. Even if the facts are wrong, in many countries a press defendant will not be found guilty unless he or she failed to fulfil the duty of checking the facts properly. After a landmark decision in the South African Supreme Court of Appeal (Bugoshi *vs* National Media Ltd and others (1996 (3) SA 78 (w)) in which it was ruled that the publication in the press of false defamatory allegations of fact will not be regarded as unlawful if, upon consideration of all circumstances of the case, it is found to have been reasonable to publish the particular facts in the particular way at the particular time. This decision, which now stands as principle in South African law, may influence the legal situation elsewhere in the region, and it implies two important ethical aspects. The first is the need for a thorough and painstaking checking and double-checking of all sources in order to ascertain as fas as possible the accuracy of the story. The other is that, once all precautions like this have been taken, then the press is free to publish as long as it is in the public interest. It is thus both a defence of the freedom of the press to be critical, and a warning to the press not to lose sight of one of its basic ethical principles.

Geoff Feltoe, professor of law at the University of Zimbabwe and a specialist in media law, reflected on the implications of laws pertaining to the media in Zimbabwe and in other southern African countries in an editorial written for *Legal Forum*, a quarterly publication of the Legal Resources Foundation and the Law Society of Zimbabwe, which was also published in *Financial Gazette* (28 January 1999).

> *In the UK and many other common law countries, truth is not a defence, although public interest may be.*

As in many other areas of law, the problem that arises with the law of defamation is how to achieve a reasonable balance between competing interests. The law must provide adequate protection against unjustifiable attacks upon reputations because such attacks on reputation can do great harm and such harm must be redressed. But the law on defamation (and various other laws) must not be applied in such a way as to stifle free debate or to prevent the media from reporting matters of public interest and concern.

Damaging story

In respect of the media, the law should provide an enabling environment for competent, professional journalism and a disabling environment for irresponsible and unprofessional journalism. Before publishing a story about another that will harm that person's reputation, the good journalist will carefully check the facts. The bad journalist will recklessly publish a damaging story without taking reasonable steps to check the correctness of the story.

In any democracy, the public will closely scrutinise the way in which leaders and other public officials are performing their duties. The public will want to know whether public officials are carrying out their duties competently and in such a way as to advance the public interest.

Public criticism

A public official who is considered to be incompetent or corrupt will attract public criticism and condemnation. The media play a vitally important role in holding public officials accountable for their actions. It is an important function of the media to probe the actions of public officials and to bring to the attention of the public any shortcomings and abuses of power by them. In Zimbabwe, however, the law of defamation and various other laws make it difficult for the press to perform this important watchdog role properly.

The law must obviously try to ensure that the watchdog does not bite the wrong people and that when the wrong people are bitten by the watchdog, the law must provide them with suitable remedies. The public interest is obviously served by the press exposing actual corruption. But it is not served by the press alleging that an official has engaged in corruption when in fact he has not done so. The public official who is falsely accused of wrongdoing suffers grave harm to his or her reputation.

Checking stories

The press is therefore expected to behave responsibly and to check its facts carefully before making allegations of wrongdoing. However, journalists face considerable difficulties in checking stories about abuses on the part of government officials, especially high-ranking officials. The task of checking would be very much easier if in Zimbabwe there was a legal obligation on the part of government ministries to supply information when they are requested by members of the public and the press to do so. At present, there is no such obligation. Not only is there no such legal obligation, but there are also ridiculously restrictive laws such as the Official Secrets Act that greatly obstruct access to official information.

Official discretion

The end result is that the supply of official information to the press is entirely dependent upon official discretion. Often requests for information are ignored or the information supplied is inadequate or the information is supplied only after a long period of time. The Ministry of Justice promised some time back that the law would be changed to allow far freer access to official information, but this has not yet happened.

Although even in systems where government departments have a legal obligation to supply information to the press, guilty officials who do not wish their wrongdoing exposed will still try to find ways of hiding away information which would establish their guilt. Concealment of damning facts is very much more difficult in such systems. Clearly, if we had such a system in Zimbabwe, a journalist would be acting unreasonably if he or she failed to use this system to check a story about alleged wrongdoing on the part of a public official.

To add to the woes of journalists, the law of defamation as it stands is very much stacked against the press. Again, the Minister of Justice has on a number of occasions promised changes, but no changes have yet occurred. If a media institution alleges wrongdoing on the part of a public official in the performance of his duties and the public official sues for defamation, the only way in which the action could be successfully defended is if the media institution proves that its allegations were true. It is no defence for the media institution to say that it believed the facts to be true and that it published the story because it believed that the public had a right to know about this matter. It is not even a defence for the media institution to establish that it took all reasonable steps to check its facts before going ahead and publishing the story.

Reliable source

Take this example. A newspaper obtains information from a reliable source within a ministry that a high-ranking person in the ministry has been taking bribes. The informant tells the newspaper that if the newspaper is sued, he will not be prepared to testify in court on behalf of the newspaper. There is no documentary evidence that can be produced in court. The newspaper does all it can to try to check the story and asks the named person to comment but he simply says that if the story is published he will sue the newspaper. If then the newspaper publishes the story and it is sued for defamation, it will be no defence that it believed the public had a right to know of the allegations of corruption and it did all that it could to verify the facts before it published the story. The effect of this is that media institutions will refrain from publishing such stories, not because they do not think the stories have substance, but because they are fearful that they would end up paying large amounts of damages because they may be unable to prove in court that the stories are true.

Dramatic change

In South Africa, until recently, the law was the same in this regard as in Zimbabwe. The position has now dramatically changed as a result of a landmark decision a few weeks ago in a case involving a defamation action against the *City Press*. In this case, the Supreme Court of Appeal stressed the democratic importance of freedom of expression and free flow of information in the society and it said it is a 'vital function of the press to make available to the community information and criticism about every aspect of public, political, social and economic activity and thus to contribute to the formation of public opinion'.

False information

The public interest, however, is not advanced by dissemination of false information. A proper balance has to be achieved between protection of reputation and freedom of speech. Making the press liable unless it could prove that what it has published is true does not achieve this balance. What it does is deter the press from publishing stories about public figures for fear that it will not be able to prove the truth of such stories in court. The court therefore decided that as the press has a duty to provide the public with information that is in the public interest, it will not be liable for defamation if it publishes information which turns out to be untrue if it was reasonable to publish those particular facts in that way at that time. A newspaper would not be liable if the press can establish that it was not negligent in publishing the information.

Clearly, in order to establish absence of negligence, the press would have to convince the court that it obtained information from a reliable source and it took reasonable steps to check the information.

In Zimbabwe, we must now move quickly to overhaul our law so as to achieve a better balance between free speech, freedom of the press and free flow of information on the one hand, and the protection of reputation on the other hand. In a recent speech, the Minister of Justice accepted that the press should be given better protection when expressing opinions about public figures. This promise must be fulfilled by the passing of appropriate legislation. If the government drags its heels on changing the law by legislation, then a suitable test case will have to be taken to our Supreme Court for a clear ruling in the light of the recent decision by the Supreme Court of Appeal in South Africa.

It must be made perfectly clear that to change our law in line with the newly established South African position would certainly not give a licence to journalists to publish false information. The foremost duty of the press is to publish correct information and they must try to do so wherever possible. But if the press decides it has an obligation to publish a story in the public interest, thinking its story is correct, but it later turns out to be incorrect, it will have a defence to a defamation action if it had done what a reasonable journalist would have done, namely that it had taken all reasonable steps to check the story before publishing it. It should also be under an obligation to retract the story and apologise as soon as it comes to light that the story is false.

An interesting scenario arises when value judgements and opinions are formulated in such a way that they may be interpreted as insulting. Here, there are clearly different practices and legal provisions in many countries. In the USA, for instance, there is no cause of action in the absence of a false statement of fact. Similarly in Sweden, value judgements can never be libellous, although when formulated in an exceptionally insulting way, they have on rare occasions been judged an affront (a special form of defamation). In other countries, truth is no defence if the insult arises from the manner in which a statement was made or disseminated, or from the circumstances in which it was made. In a few countries, courts tend to treat statements that primarily involve value judgments but have a factual basis – for example, obvious hyperbole – as factual statements requiring proof of truth or journalistic care. In several countries, public interest is a defence to insulting opinions. Opinions in the context of political debate, especially when made against a politician or other public figure, are subject to particular protection. Moreover, insulting expressions of opinion are more likely to be tolerated when made in response to a personal attack. 'Fair comment' is often a defence if it is based, in good faith, on a factual foundation that is true and is set out either in the publication itself or referred to with sufficient clarity.

In several countries, plaintiffs who are public officials, politicians and/or other public figures are required to meet a higher standard of proof, either de facto or in law, for both falsehoods and critical opinions. Several countries use the concept 'public figure', although the category's parameters are often not well defined. In France, for example, the category is defined as 'persons performing a public function', which includes ministers, members of parliament, civil servants and any public agent or person performing a public duty, even on a temporary basis, such as a juror or a witness. In practice, political leaders who do not fall into one of the specified categories are also held to a higher standard.

The most developed 'public figure' doctrine may be found in USA case law. It defines 'public figures' as either those who occupy positions of such influence that they must be regarded as public figures for all purposes; or those who have thrust themselves to the forefront of particular public controversies in order to influence the outcome of the issues and, thus, are public figures for the purposes of those specific controversies only. Like public officials, public figures invite the comment to which they are exposed and have access to the media to counteract false statements.

Swedish law is unusual in that companies, organisations and government authorities have no right to initiate libel actions. Consequently, the press enjoys great freedom in scrutinising and criticising government, businesses and other institutions. The press, however, has a professional ethical obligation under the voluntary Press Code to grant institutions a right of reply to factual statements made about them.

In most countries, the primary difference between criminal and civil actions concerns the remedies available. In some, while a plaintiff in a criminal action may be entitled to claim compensation for non-material damage (pain and suffering), the amount that may be awarded is usually limited by statute. In contrast, in other countries, a plaintiff in a civil action may be able to recover only for actual damage (loss of business), but the amount generally is not limited by statute. In some countries, plaintiffs can recover for immaterial damages too. In most European countries, damages, while higher than criminal fines, are relatively modest, even in cases involving major public figures. Awards are highest in the UK, where they often reach hundreds of thousands of pounds, and in the USA, where successful plaintiffs have been awarded millions of dollars.

In most civil law countries, plaintiffs can also receive non-monetary relief, such as a right of reply, retraction, correction, publication of a court judgment, or prohibition of further publication. While the laws of some countries permit up to a year's imprisonment for defamation, no one in a European country has been imprisoned for defamation in recent memory.

In Sweden, only one person, the 'responsible editor' designated by the owner, may be held liable, and is held strictly liable irrespective of whether he or she has read the offensive publication. This arrangement has at least two advantages: it ensures that one person with resources can always be held liable, and it provides security for all others involved in the publication process. However, in the UK, journalists, distributors and even printers may be sued. This is also the case in countries following the principles of British law, such as African common law countries.

Despite the powerful US case law, which makes it difficult for public figures to win defamation actions, public figures bring defamation actions, and win, at approximately the same rate as other plaintiffs. Despite the significant awards, they are generally dwarfed by the enormous costs of defending these actions, and the successful party (as in virtually all civil actions) cannot recover costs. Win or lose, press defendants inevitably are economic losers, and surveys show that the possibility of defamation actions constitutes a substantial disincentive for covering certain kinds of stories, especially by small- and medium-sized publications. The possibility of defamation actions similarly exerts a strong chilling effect when costs and awards are also high, and thus it is linked to important ethical questions of checking sources, but also daring to publish in spite of the risks when it is in the public interest.

In most countries, the costs of bringing a lawsuit are sufficiently high to discourage all but the well to do. However, even in countries where public figures may carry a heavier burden of proof, the bulk of cases are initiated by public figures. In such countries, the defamation laws (and where they exist, privacy laws) primarily serve to protect the rich and/or powerful.

In countries where press councils handle most defamation complaints, few reach the courts, damages are low, and the press does not complain that defamation actions negatively affect its activities. This pattern seems to suggest that the high costs associated with defending defamation actions may be more of a deterrent to investigative reporting than laws favouring plaintiffs.

GOVERNMENT CENSORSHIP/SELF-CENSORSHIP

Since the early 1990s, there have been numerous calls for the institutionalisation of the freedom of expression and of the media, without qualifications, to be included in national constitutions and in the African Charter on Human Rights. An important event in this context was the establishment of the Media Institute of Southern Africa (MISA) in August 1992,[20] which has independent media institutions from the entire southern African region as members, and is an outcome of the Windhoek Declaration of 3 May 1991 on 'promoting an independent and pluralistic African press'. MISA's first objective is 'to promote and defend press freedom and take appropriate steps where such freedoms are violated and to seek to remove obstacles and impediments to the free flow of information'. Furthermore, the declaration states: 'African states should be encouraged to provide constitutional guarantees of the freedom of the press and freedom of association'. This interest in the ideals and the reality of the principle of freedom of expression arises from both a concrete historical situation and a philosophical tradition of arguments for the freedom of expression in relation to the role of the state.

The experiences in many African and other Third World countries have shown that State control over the media has an institutional aspect in the form of direct or indirect ownership of the media, or content control, ranging from outright censorship to other types of interference in what the media present to their audiences. This is often linked to control and direct coercion over the media practitioners themselves, ranging from possible economic and social sanctions to outright liquidations, and often results in widespread self-censorship. These practices originate to a large degree in a fear among government officials and politicians of having corrupt and oppressive practices exposed publicly, and apprehension of losing their power if free public debate were to be allowed.[21] It is indicative of the situation in Africa – with the exception of South Africa – that the discussion of what free media entails has been concentrated around State control. Virtually no attention has been given to commercial control of the media.

Discussions with practising journalists in Africa reveal that there is a widespread assumption that there are far more stringent limitations to what may be written than is really the case, and that the media organisations themselves have found this to be an easy way round the dilemmas raised by modern, hard-hitting critical journalism. It is not so much the political powers that restrict African journalism and makes it fall back on 'ministerial speech reporting', but rather internalised assumptions of what is expected of the media. It is, of course, a far simpler form of journalism to practice than proper, critical, investigative reporting. Paradoxically, the practice of self-censorship may function as an excuse for not checking stories properly, or for taking on the often cumbersome and not very exciting work of following up leads. This again is linked to the poor training that many journalists have received and their often low social standing. By this, we are not indicating that self-censorship may not be based on a very real fear of reprisals from government and other powers. The intention is to illustrate how self-imposed regulations emanating from real or imagined threats often function as efficiently as formalised forms of censorship. There are examples where self-censorship has led to the relaxation of overt censorship.

CULTURAL CONTEXTS

Kaarle Nordenstreng[22] writes about the tradition of media ethics in relation to general ethics and points out that media ethics in *Media Ethics: Cases and Moral Reasoning* (Christians, et al., 1995)[23] is defined by five principles:

(1) Aristotle's Golden Mean: 'Moral virtue is the appropriate location between two extremes'; (2) Kant's Categorical Imperative: 'Act on that maxim which you will to become a universal law'; (3) Mill's Principle of Utility: 'Seek the greatest happiness for the greatest number'; (4) Rawls's Veil of Ignorance: 'Justice emerges when negotiating without social differentiations'; (5) Judeo-Christian Persons as Ends: 'Love your neighbour as yourself'.

Even if these guidelines have their roots in a distinctly Western tradition of ethics, there are also universal principles. The world is not a composite of completely disjointed cultures and values; there also is cohesion. However, the question is: What are these universal principles? In relation to media ethics, three areas of concern have been suggested: a quest for truth (accuracy, objectivity, etc.); a desire for responsibility (justice, equality, etc.); and a call for free expression (free flow, lack of censorship, etc.). To these might be added normative universal principles based on the preservation of nature, life and human solidarity.

A commitment to universal principles, however, does not eliminate all differences and suggests that normative ethics grounded in human dignity are pluralistic. This also applies to 'truth', which is understood as authenticity in a social context rather than as a strict correspondence to static reality. This implies a search for fundamental values cutting across cultures and throughout the ecosystem.

There are two other intellectual challenges of a general nature raised by the theme of media ethics. The first is the dilemma of individualism versus communal values. While ethics by its very nature invites us to consider an individual conscience, it is necessary to refer to the social and community setting of the individual. The second dilemma is that of regulation – freedom versus control. Professional media ethics is seen as a substitute for official regulation by law and the state. Voluntary regulatory bodies in the form of media councils and codes of conduct are also a form of regulation, which have as their base a system of agreements between the parties of the communication process. These should be implemented, taking into consideration the values of specific cultures in relation to universal ethical norms.

EDITORIAL RESPONSIBILITY[24]

There is one sacrosanct editorial rule: the editor-in-chief is outwardly responsible for what appears in his or her newspaper, is broadcast over his or her radio, or transmitted over his or her television channel. If staff make mistakes, overstep ethical boundaries, write libellous articles, or a story is the result of gross negligence on the part of a reporter or sub-editor, it is the editor-in-chief who is responsible, whether he or she was involved in the production of the item or not. To some degree, this safeguards editorial independence, but it is also a precarious responsibility.

Journalism is suspect if editorial judgements are not made freely and independently by journalists on the ground, by editorial teams or by trusted editors. Journalists in countries recently emerged from authoritarian control, for instance in Eastern Europe, are passionate about the independence of journalists. After decades of restriction, they are inclined to see any restrictive editorial act from a 'boss' as a disgraceful interference; a boss is any supervisor who does not normally make detailed editorial decisions. Exasperated journalists share this attitude in systems long used to freedom, when a chief sub, senior producer or editor overrules them. The majority of decisions are made by the reporters who gather the news, by the subs who prepare it for the page, or by the producers who finalise it for the programme. Most editorial machines could not work in any other way; decisions are normally made and applied at this level. At times, however, the norm has to give way to senior editorial staff who have the authority to intervene.

Newspaper editors fight vigorously for their right to edit. They often seek assurances from proprietors and controlling interests that they will not be interfered with. At the same time, they devolve responsibility downwards, to their editorial staff. Sometimes editorial independence is doubted. Doubts of this kind are often voiced and equally often denied about editors of newspapers owned by multinational media conglomerates, such as Rupert Murdoch's News Corporation. Whatever terms and assurances prevail, even the most independent newspaper editors are not free to do whatever they wish; they have to operate within the established position of their newspapers. For those editors given assurances of independence, the theory is that owners choose them to do what is required by the established editorial approach of the newspaper and leave them to it until the confidence of the owners evaporates, at which point the editors are sacked. The theory accords reasonably with the reality, on the understanding that even the best owners nudge their editors now and again.

The problems and structures in broadcasting are less clear. A newspaper editor could scrutinise all important editorial columns, and, in some newspapers, every editorial word, before publication. Higher bosses in broadcasting organisations cannot possibly vet all speech programmes before broadcast. Even if they could, they would still have the problem of how to supervise live programmes that are not scripted. The director general of the British Broadcasting Corporation (BBC) used to be referred to as the 'editor-in-chief'; and director generals of broadcasting corporations and companies, and their senior managers are members of editors' associations in, for example, the Scandinavian countries. This nevertheless implies that their editorial responsibility can be discharged, only exceptionally, at critical moments in certain editorial issues. The reality of being editor-in-chief is not available either to managing directors of independent radio stations, regional television stations and channel controllers. None may exercise the degree of editorial oversight to justify the description 'editor'; at best, they are called in on special problems. Editorial authority devolves, of necessity, to programme editors and producers, and the ordinary toilers in the newsrooms, at the programme editorial desks and in the cutting rooms.

MEDIA AND COMMERCIALISM

So far, we have dealt with the media in relation to principles and rights, focusing on media systems, theories of democracy, legal frameworks and conflict with government. However, there is more at stake – the economics of the media. All media is dependent upon financing; most are business enterprises aimed at making money. Most radio and television programmes are financed through advertising and, from a commercial point of view, the programmes exist in order to obtain an audience for such advertising. The exceptions are the public service broadcasting corporations, such as the BBC, because they are paid for by alternative means – through licence fees and government grants. To some degree, they have been insulated from a strong commercial imperative, but public service broadcasting has increasingly become subject to commercial pressures. Many public service broadcasters receive an increasing part of their funding from advertising. This, for example, is the case with the South African Broadcasting Corporation (SABC) in South Africa.

This raises some important problems because, as argued earlier, there is a strong tradition that the media, and particularly the news media, should be free of government control. But what about freedom from commercial pressures? Does the combination of broadcasters being dependent on the State through licence fees determined by parliament, government grants, and dependence on advertisers, pose a double threat to media independence?

Arguments about commercial interests and media independence are often formulated on the basis of historical references. The argument is often based on that fact that the commercial success of newspapers in Europe in the nineteenth century gave them the independence and power to criticise government. It is also argued that there is a link between the financial health of the press and good journalism. Newspapers need a sound economic basis to be able to pay for experienced and sufficient journalists, who have special skills to cover domestic and foreign news, and provide coverage of all areas, and those who cover special interests, such as cultural features, to have the resources to pursue investigations over a period of time.

... the question of whether commercial pressures inhibit the freedom of the media is central to international media debates.

Still, the question of whether commercial pressures inhibit the freedom of the media is central to international media debates. Those who defend the free market argue that it is a necessary condition for democracy to flourish. They say that market arrangements encourage a diversity of opinion and best serve the democratic need for informed citizens. They also argue that the market is the best institutional arrangement for ensuring that the press can act as a check on government.

The appeal of the market is stronger in situations where the media appear weak in relation to the apparent might of the state. The markets for media are, with some exceptions, small, weak and poorly developed in southern Africa. Entrepreneurs, journalist cooperatives and media-dedicated businesspeople, mostly back the market media.

Consequently, private media are not controlled by oligopolies as they are internationally and in the North. What exists outside South Africa are small and underdeveloped media businesses, comprising mostly magazines, smaller book publishers and maybe a newspaper. It is indicative that the largest media group in Zimbabwe is the government-controlled Zimbabwe Mass Media Trust.

However, the market is vulnerable, and from this perspective, the central financial role of advertising in the media is particularly interesting. In underdeveloped markets in general, close relationships between the private sector and the State, and the existence of many parastatals, as in southern Africa, the direct editorial influence exerted by advertisers through the granting or withholding of advertising support for ideological reasons may be considerable. It creates pressure on editors and media proprietors to accommodate or anticipate advertisers' ideological concerns, which is a very real threat to media independence. In Zimbabwe, there have been allegations of both advertisers withdrawing substantial campaigns from newspapers that printed stories that are critical of them, and of reluctance on the part of newspapers to publish stories revealing malpractice in the private sector for fear of being victimised economically.

Another important question is the influence of owners on their newspapers, and whether their business goals affect their editorial activities. How much influence would be acceptable? Should they be involved at all? Is it acceptable for them to make suggestions about content, but no more?

Another argument is that the market undermines the relationship between journalism and democracy. Journalism values often conflict with the requirements of the market place. It is alleged that, to survive in the marketplace, the press has to satisfy its customers' preferences. In other words, the press gives its readers only what they want, and the more competitive the market, the greater the pressure to deliver sensationalism. Fierce competition may also erode professional ethics.

There are, however, two phenomena that reflect the economic pressures on the media more than any others: first, the trend towards concentration of ownership; and second, the influence of advertising and marketing.

OWNERSHIP AND PRESSURE FROM COMMERCIAL INTERESTS

Since the beginning of the twentieth century, there has been a distinct development in the direction of large media groups and the concentration of ownership of the media, initially in the USA and in the UK, but globally since the 1970s. This development is clearly linked to new media technologies, both in the form of satellites and cable, and in the digitalisation of the media. Global cultural and media corporations transcend the divisions between the various media. They control book publishing, the music industry, film and television, in a global economic environment of enormous opportunities and escalating costs, where there is a clear relation between size and power. What we are seeing in the development of the cultural industries is the importance of size, and this gives rise to an explosion of mergers, new acquisitions and strategic alliances.

The merger of Time-Warner and Ted Turner's broadcasting corporation CNN created the world's biggest media empire, until it was merged in 2000 with America On Line to create a media conglomerate that really combined a content producer and a company with a delivery network of immense importance. This merger is a sign of the convergent media empires that are about to develop. The earlier fusion of Disney and ABC was a step in the direction of this new convergence in media economies and technologies. From its original involvement in consumer electronic hardware, Sony has diversified into cultural software through the acquisitions of CBS and Columbia Pictures, which constitute a total entertainment business, and the company's long-term strategy is to use the control over both hardware and software industries to dominate the market for the next generation of audiovisual products. Rupert Murdoch's News Corporation has rapidly moved from its base in newspapers into the audiovisual sector (Sky Channel and BskyB.) Through its acquisition of Fox Broadcasting, 20th Century Fox, and Manchester United Football Club, the company strives to be involved at all levels of production and distribution of entertainment programmes, and news and sports coverage in all media, from print to electronic. Murdoch's Star TV in Hong Kong transmits across the four time zones in which half of the world's population lives. Then there is the strategy behind Microsoft's plans to control the world's digital networks and products. The same processes of integration take place on national and regional levels. One example is the way international media corporations have combined with South African media capital to use South Africa as a stepping-stone for expansion into the rest of the African continent. M-Net's growth into Africa and the Middle East is a case in point.

Satellite footprints cover the world and represent a serious challenge to the possibility of establishing a democratic world system of communication. Interpreted pessimistically, we may be moving to an information context that is not about giving people access to a variety of information and entertainment, but rather the widest possible distribution of limited forms of media products. The aim is to overcome national boundaries and open up the 'free flow' of information across a world market. The openness is positive, but within this changed order driven by economic and entrepreneurial imperatives, the public is no longer addressed as citizens, but rather as economic objects, as consumers. The basis of the traditional public service ethos in promoting democracy and public life are regarded as factors inhibiting the advancement of new media markets. The worst possible scenario is where there exists a modus vivendi or common interests between the stakes of the conglomerates and the agenda of authoritarian governments that control national majority media. A striking example of this is the deal between Murdoch's Star TV and the Chinese government, which effectively bars the Chinese audience from receiving critical news about their situation.

... programme formats developed in the USA have created the framework for television productions in most other countries.

It is tempting to analyse these developments on the basis of a theory of media imperialism and cultural dependency, which may be illustrated by referring to the world pattern of international television flows. The USA is the world's biggest television exporter. It 'exports' a greater quantity of television programmes than all other nations combined, and imports only between one and two per cent of its television programmes. This pattern of American dominance is particularly pronounced in such crucial areas of television programming as prime-time fiction and news. World news is, for example, largely supplied by a very small number of news agencies, all of which are Anglo-American, and clearly shape the international political agenda by the way in which they define values and select which issues are worthy of attention. Furthermore, programme formats developed in the USA have created the framework for televisions productions in most other countries.

There are many aspects to these analyses; they grasp systematic patterns, but may be criticised for being too simplistic and mechanical. They tend to focus exclusively on the pattern of American television exports, without giving sufficient attention to non-American forms of cultural dominance, involving, for example, the continuing export of cultural materials by British and French media producers to ex-colonies in Africa, the strength of Mexico as a television exporter to other Latin American countries, and the position of Brazil, which exports tele-novellas to southern Europe and elsewhere (e.g. Lusophone Africa). Brazil even outperforms countries such as France in the world market for programmes. The Brazilian cultural industry has its genesis in a big national market for cultural goods. It is characterised by a mixture of the modern and the traditional, as witnessed by a remarkable blend of mass and popular cultures. The products of Brazil's competitive television industry combine elements of high modernity and signs of the pre-industrial.

Critics of the cultural imperialism theory argue that it presumes a hypodermic model of media effects, which is a metaphor for how the media are perceived to directly influence their audiences. It assumes that the impact of viewing American televisual material on audiences across the world can be automatically predicted. Empirical analyses and research in this field demonstrate not so much the direct effects of American media material, as the capacity of audiences in different situations to reinterpret the American-produced material in ways influenced by their local circumstances. There is no doubt that American popular culture holds a fascination that transcends cultural borders, and that audiences are not forced to consume American popular culture; they do it voluntarily, and enjoy what they see and hear. This should not lead to the conclusion that cultural power does not exist, or that the American-dominated media products have no effect, but should suggest that the modes in which cultural power is both exercised and resisted are complex.

Arguments about threats of media concentration may be summarised by way of three main concerns. The first concern is that the views of the few owners in the field will be imposed. This could result in fewer viewpoints being expressed or an increasing similarity between the viewpoints that are expressed. However, it may be argued that media concentration in itself may result in a better product (for example, there may be a greater economic use of resources). In addition, while there is evidence that the ownership of the media is concentrated in the hands of a few capitalists, there is limited evidence demonstrating that this affects the content of the media.

A second concern is that many media institutions are owned by corporations that have no commitment to the qualities of journalism, and find that they can get more profit for less quality – for example, by reducing the number of journalists.

A third concern about the concentration of media ownership is that of companies expanding into different areas. The Time-Warner grouping links a predominantly entertainment-focused company (Warner) with a news one (Time) and a digital delivery network (AOL). For example, the news arm may be tempted, in news and reviews, to deal favourably with the entertainment company's films. Another example is that a company's newspapers may not investigate the activities of other companies in the business group to which it belongs.

Newspapers have also been used to pursue commercial vendettas. A frequent source of concern in the UK has been Rupert Murdoch. In the debate over his role and influence, it has been argued both in the press and in scholarly media critique that his formula for media success was to narrow the editorial focus of his tabloids, concentrate on sex and crime (although this has always been part of other newspapers), reduce news coverage, and increase chequebook journalism. As proprietor, he can remove and appoint editors to present his views. What makes this even more worrying is that Murdoch owns a number of media outlets. Will his newspapers give favourable reviews to the books published by the company he owns? A specific case in point is that a Murdoch-owned publishing house refused to publish the book written by that last British Governor in Hong Kong, Chris Patten, because the book was critical of Chinese politics and this was seen as a threat to Murdoch's business interests in China.

Internationally, one of the consequences of this type of changing patterns of ownership is that media enterprises have sometimes refrained from criticising or investigating the activities of the giant conglomerates to which they belong. In exceptional cases, parent companies have even stepped in to suppress indirect criticism of their interests. The free market thus compromises rather than guarantees the editorial integrity of commercial media, and impairs in particular its scrutiny of private corporate power. More importantly, changes in media ownership have affected its relationship with government. Media conglomerates may be seen as independent power centres that use their political leverage to pursue corporate gain. Media conglomerates are not independent watchdogs serving public interest, but self-seeking, corporate mercenaries using their muscle to promote private interests.

Domination of the press by large media companies has another detrimental effect – that of making it difficult for new entrants into the industry or for smaller, independent newspapers to survive. Large companies can buy or squeeze out smaller titles, restricting diversity.

In Europe (both nationally and within the framework of the EU), there have been attempts to curb concentrations of media ownership, by setting limits for cross-media ownership and ensuring that no media proprietor owns a monopoly of media within an industry sector either nationally or within a region.

An interesting illustration of how new media capital and particularly foreign media capital may change the situation in a country was the launch of a new newspaper group in Zimbabwe in 1998.[25] The company behind the initiative, Associated Newspapers of Zimbabwe (ANZ (Pvt) Ltd), first launched five local newspapers that all turned out not to be economically viable. Then, in April 1999, ANZ launched its flagship, the *Daily News*, which, in the beginning, had economic and administrative problems, but after having managed against great opposition from, among others, government circles to both establish a good organisational framework for its paper, and creating a hard-hitting independent newspaper, it became a serious competitor to the government-controlled *The Herald*. In 2000, it overtook *The Herald* in circulation. The *Daily News* had its offices bombed once, and its printing press was also blown up. In spite of this and other forms of continuous harassment and sabotage from ZANU(PF) circles, it has continued to be the main voice of independent reporting in Zimbabwe. One of the reasons for this may be found in the editorial principle behind the paper, as formulated on its website. These principles read as a good guideline for journalistic ethics:

> ANZ will be independent of any political, commercial or sectional obligations or commitments, and will not represent the interests of any one section of the population at the expense of another. It will strive to ensure there is no discrimination on the basis of race, gender, religion, ethnic group, sexual orientation or any physical attribute.
>
> Reports shall be fair, balanced and accurate, and diversity of opinion shall be encouraged.
>
> Errors of fact shall be speedily and prominently corrected.
>
> The privacy of individuals shall be fully respected, except in instances of demonstrable public interest.
>
> Fact and opinion shall be clearly separated and identified.
>
> Reports of a sensitive nature will be handled with great care to ensure that the rights of free speech and a free press do not diminish any other basic human rights, nor directly incite feelings of contempt, hatred or aggression.
>
> Great care will be taken to ensure that reports on events which might be deemed by a reasonable person to be of a lewd or salacious nature are sensitively handled and are only used if they can be shown to be in the public interest. The same applies to reports which might be deemed to encourage crime or violence. Full cognisance will be taken of the fact that media products are used by children.
>
> In addition to co-operating fully with independent self-regulatory bodies, ANZ's newspapers will, wherever practicable, appoint and pay for a Readers' Ombudsman to represent the interests of readers.

One of the most interesting aspects of ANZ was the way that its capital base was established. It consisted of investments from interested parties in Zimbabwe and foreign capital. It is no secret that the company has had economic problems during its existence. This is partly due to the unwise investment in the local newspapers, as well as a certain degree of under capitalisation at the start. However, ANZ has survived and its ownership structure is a good example of how the market can further media diversity.

What is particularly interesting is that foreign media capital is providing the impetus for greater media pluralism in Zimbabwe. However, this aspect has also provoked a worrying response from the Zimbabwean government. Both the Minister of Information, Chen Chimutengwende, and the Minister of Industry and Commerce, Nathan Shamuayirira, criticised the project for being foreign dominated, for having the potential to destabilise the political order, and of furthering oppositional political agendas. In early 1999, Chimutengwende stated in parliament that he was considering introducing rules against foreign investment in Zimbabwean media and restricting the right of international donors to support media in the country. The threats were realised in the proposed Access to Information Act in late 2001, where it was stated that foreign nationals and companies were prohibited from owning mass media operations. One of the interesting aspects of these developments is that it illustrates, to an extent, that the market media in Africa are independent.

From an international perspective, however, integrating regional media into media businesses based in South Africa, whether they are South African-owned or part of larger international media corporations, may signify implications other than diversity. This may include the development of local monopolies and media chains controlling the press, book and magazine publishing, and electronic media. The situation in South Africa, with the parallel development of both black empowerment, and concentration and cross ownership of the media industry, is a very interesting phenomenon in this context.[26] Here, one sees development where previous ideological contradictions are broken, international capital is moving in, and the control of the media is, to a considerable degree, being regrouped, with core sectors of finance and industrial capital being joined by black interests. The previously Afrikaans-dominated media chains Naspers and Perskor, and the previously English-dominated Argus Group and Times Media, have entered into alliances with new capital, much of which is based in black trade union pension funds and has close connections with the African National Congress (ANC). It is thus possible to see the development of new alliances between old industrial and mining capital, Afrikaans capital interests, and new political interests in the restructuring of the South African media. In addition, there is growing international interest in the country's media. For example, Irish media investor, Tony O'Reilly, plays a central role in Independent Newspapers (previously the Argus group of newspapers).

Both from a southern African and an international perspective, the development trends discussed above raise two important questions about the place of the media in a broad discussion of media diversity, which is linked to central problems in media ethics: Firstly, how important is media pluralism for a fully free press? Perhaps the question should not be judged in terms of the number of viewpoints. What of factors such as the truth or falsity of information, differences in validity and sophistication of the views expressed, or the superficiality or thoroughness of the messages presented?

Secondly, has there really been a decline in media outlets? This leads to another question: How is media pluralism measured? Media pluralism can be judged by the number of publications and broadcast outlets in the marketplace, the nature of the ownership of these outlets, and the characteristics of the content (programming and news) they deliver. The assumption is that the more outlets from different ownerships there are available, the better. While there has been increasing centralisation of ownership, there has also been an increase in the number of outlets in the proliferation of cable and satellite television channels, and magazines available. There are diverse opinions in book publishing too. It can be argued that the pluralism of the system is growing, but the real problem may be shrinkage of media providing news, and restriction of pluralism or diversity in journalism.

ADVERTISING AND MARKETING

It is worth repeating that the development of modern media has, as its point of departure, the development of the market for mass-produced commodities and the development of mass democracy based on the principle of all citizens having the right to vote in free elections. Given such a perspective, it is possible to argue that it was advertising that gave the press financial independence in the nineteenth century and thus freedom from political interests. The media provide information and entertainment to their audiences, based on what the public wants, but also provide advertisers with a market for their products. In other words, the media provide consumers. A dilemma for television is: does commercial television exist to bring programmes to viewers, or to deliver viewers to advertisers? In fact, this is a dilemma for all media; newspapers, magazines, and most broadcasting could not exist without advertising.

The amount of advertising income determines the amount of space available for editorial material, and therefore affects the content and structure of the newspaper or programme. Certain types of coverage in newspapers are often linked to specialised advertising – for example, fashion reportage, which is linked to advertisements for clothing, or special motor pages linked to advertisements for cars. Of course, there are many specialist magazines where editorial content and advertising are closely interconnected – for example, motoring magazines. Magazines or newspapers may create special supplements to attract specialised advertising – for example, a focus on a particular country by an international business magazine that attracts advertising from major companies in that country.

The difference between a valid editorial mention of a commercial product and a plug can be so fine that even the most experienced do not necessarily realise the difference.

One of the most contentious areas in this context concerns plugging and/or product placement. While promoters work energetically and inventively to get product placement by mention, reporters, editors and programme producers are expected to make sure that they do not include references that promote products in their copy or programmes. Ever-present temptations range from the frequently fallen-for sponsored survey, which is usually trivial and hardly ever worthwhile as a statistical statement, to crediting a commercial body for a sponsored event. Sponsored events are becoming increasingly frequent, particularly in television and for sports events, and there seems to be no editorial escape.

News and current affairs programmes on television are less prone to product placement than drama and other creative works. When products are shown, it is easier to make sure they are justified editorially. Factual programmes and newspaper pages that feature commercial goods as a matter of course, such as those about food, holidays and motoring, can only ensure that they publicise a reasonable range without favouritism. The difference between a valid editorial mention of a commercial product and a plug can be so fine that even the most experienced do not necessarily realise the difference. To plug a book is acceptable, usually. To plug a film or a play is tolerated, often. Books, films and plays are given special treatment because they are entertainment or have cultural value. For programmes and newspapers, they also provide lively content, interviews with famous or unusual authors, and comments on and from notable actors. The different media go hand in glove, each doing the other a few favours for the benefit of the public. To plug a car may be done in context; new cars are reviewed and talked about in much the same way as cultural products – probably because they are regarded as glamorous, rather than dirty and damaging to the environment. Separating advertisers' interests and feature or editorial material can be quite tenuous in the specialist magazine press (consumer, style, hobby and leisure magazines).

While this area is full of ethical issues, there appears to be no clear logic. However, it is extremely important that the principle of clearly separating editorial and advertising is maintained, and that advertisers in no way influence journalistic content. If this division is not maintained, the media risk losing independence and may be accused of not upholding one of the most basic of ethical media considerations, that editorial decisions are not influenced by outside forces.

Newspapers and other news media can be affected by advertising in several ways. First, newspapers may be led to increase the ratio of advertising to editorial content in their products. Second, they may allow market criteria (how many advertisers will be attracted, or what kind of audience may be provided for the advertiser) to determine new ventures. Marketing may also affect media content; in the fight for profits, it is considered an essential tool. Editors and news directors are expected to package their news and information to attract a target audience. In newspapers, this has led to an increasing percentage of space being devoted to 'soft' news or features, or lifestyle journalism, such as articles on travel and recreation. This dilemma is particularly important in relation to television ratings. Nevertheless, do the media have an ethical obligation to provide coverage of all significant segments of their geographical area, whether they make money from them or not? Third, print media may accept editorial-style adverts (advertorials). These are supplements paid for by advertisers but look like the editorial pages; they resemble independent feature articles, but are in fact advertising. Fourth, news media may suppress stories in protest when advertisers withdraw their support, or suppress them in case they might. Fifth, the media may provide lowest-common-factor content aimed at the largest audience. Sixth, newspapers and magazines may provide news space for companies proportionate to the advertising they buy.

Editors and news directors are expected to package their news and information to attract a target audience.

One of the most problematic developments in international news media, and particularly in popular newspapers, is that they themselves have become commodities that must be aggressively marketed. Thus, the rise of what has been called campaign journalism around particularly contentious issues may, to a significant degree, be seen as the result not of market research done by marketing consultants but journalistic decisions. The use of marketing techniques by the press has the justification that editors and reporters are not representative of their readers and listeners; market research information gives media organisations a continuous source of feedback from readers and listeners. A marketing approach to news is the most effective and efficient way to select and present news that is of interest and pertinent to the audience. This leads to editors no longer determining what their audiences need or should have. Rather, they provide the news the audiences say they want, as interpreted through the results obtained by market researchers. The question is: Who should decide what is news – the editor or someone apart from journalism – that is, the marketing department of the media conglomerate? This potentially undermines the principles of editorial independence and leads to the old debate of whether the press should give readers what marketers think they want or what editors think they need.

THE BASICS OF JOURNALISM AND ETHICS

Ideally, one of the powers of the media is to act as a check against government, and to defend public interest by uncovering abuses of power in private and corporate enterprises. But the media, which always hold others to account, themselves accountable? And if so, to whom?

One of the more practical aspects to this question is whether there are mechanisms for public feedback and criticism? Should there be a 'right to reply' when the media make a mistake or wrong individual citizens? Do newspapers and broadcasters allow enough space or time for people to respond?

Strong believers in the principle of a market-based media freedom doctrine argue a model of accountability throughout the marketplace. They would claim that, as far as the media are held accountable to forces outside the media market, their freedom is necessarily diminished. The argument is that, through the marketplace, the public rewards or punishes the media by buying or not buying (the newspaper, magazine or book), viewing or not viewing (the television programme), listening or not listening to (the radio programme). However, the market model assumes a knowledgeable and concerned audience with a certain purchasing power, and is based on a belief that, when people know the good, they will see it, and that when they know the bad, they will avoid it. However, this is a large assumption if the audience is passive and the choice of available media is limited, either because the market is small (as in many African societies), or the market has been undermined by concentrations of media ownership, which restrict the choices available (as in many northern societies).

An alternative way of dealing with accountability is through self-regulation and the use of media councils. However, as codes and councils are often formed by professionals for professionals, accountability may develop into only being an in-house matter. The problem here is whether internal self-regulation can be effective in providing accountability, or whether it is a screen behind which the media carry on much as before. In particular, there is the issue of whether such councils and codes have any force to implement their decisions, and whether the media and the public they are supposed to serve take their decisions seriously. This depends on the legitimacy and respect they have in the media fraternity and among the public. To give them no power or bestow limited legitimacy seems tantamount to avoiding accountability on the part of the media.

PROFESSIONALISM AND CODES OF CONDUCT[27]

It is interesting that journalists and organisations that believe in the independence of the media voluntarily impose a code of ethics upon themselves. This may be said to curtail their absolute freedom of expression. Journalists and their organisations therefore believe that freedom and responsibility, or independence of the media and media ethics, are closely connected. Codes of press conduct, apart from restricting certain immoral practices on the part of journalists, have another function – to safeguard press freedom itself. In this sense, media ethics becomes a guarantee for media independence. It is for this reason that press codes, for example, commit journalists to protecting confidential sources of information. It is common for the most important leaks about government misconduct

Journalists working for the tabloids often see the codes as hindering their 'investigations' ...

and scandals to come from sources inside government. These sources would cease and major disclosures in the public interest would no longer take place if such sources could not trust journalists to uphold this section of their ethical code. This particular clause in codes of conduct has a direct bearing on access to information and, therefore, on press freedom.

Journalistic codes of conduct or ethical codes may be viewed from three perspectives, linked to specific historical and cultural contexts:

Firstly, they have been seen and developed as part of a process giving journalism a professional status; as part of an increasing self-awareness by journalists that they belong to a profession with its own set of rules, forms of education and learning. These codes contribute to the setting of standards among a group of professional people whose esteem and self-esteem have often been quite low. This perspective was prominent in Europe and the USA when the first codes of conduct were introduced between the late-nineteenth century and the Second World War. In many ways, the codes grew out of a need for common ethical grounds in a situation of liability and unclear frameworks, when the journalistic profession was regarded with suspicion by authorities and held in low esteem by the public. Consequently, it is a perspective that is linked to situations when the media and journalism are in a state of change and under pressure. The need to adopt ethical codes may also be seen as part of the professional organisational process among journalists. It is characteristic that the formulation and adoption of ethical codes is now taking place in many Third World countries and in the new democracies in Eastern Europe, signifying an important element in the struggle for democratic media structures.

Secondly, there exists an attitude to media ethics that regards codes of conduct as nothing but a form of rhetorical principles that cover up blatant and increasingly cynical media that, in reality, break every ethical rule it pronounces. From such a perspective, codes of conduct are seen as nothing but relics from the past as they are constantly changed and undermined by forms of journalism appealing to low morals, and entirely dependent on commercial interests. The ethical principles that are found in the codes are increasingly regarded as a cover for journalistic practice that undermines them. This is a perspective frequently put forward by media critics in Western societies with highly commercial media, and where so-called 'tabloid' journalism is a prominent feature of the media scene – not only in newspapers, but also in other media. Journalists working for the tabloids often see the codes as hindering their 'investigations' into, for example, the private lives of prominent citizens.

Discussions about upholding ethical codes often take the form of debates within the journalistic community, where representatives of the so-called 'quality media' demand respect for ethical standards and those who represent popular or tabloid journalism maintain the need for changing and more relaxed standards. Alternatively, the debate on the one hand takes place between a concerned public, often represented by politicians, and media proprietors and editors on the other. The demands from the public and the politicians frequently involve imposing ethical restrictions on the media, often through legal means. While the media defends the freedom of the market, it also has recourse to arguments of freedom of expression and the public's right to know. Ethical principles, rights arguments and commercial interests thus are being brought together in forms that make it very difficult to separate one argument from another. Examples of these attitudes were found in the debates in the UK about paparazzi journalism after the death of Diana, Princess of Wales.

Ethical codes can also be viewed as a mechanism for self-regulation that protects the media from intervention from outside forces, and protects the public from irresponsible journalism.

Ethical codes form one of many foundations for free and accountable media, with self-regulation an increasingly important form of 'control'. Given this perspective, the issue is not journalism as such, but pertains to democracy as a system for governing society. Media in the contemporary world have become so vital that there are indeed good reasons to discuss and establish norms for ethical practice.

The codes of ethics that exist in many parts of the world have some common features:

- A basic, universal model of journalistic codes is developing, with the accent on truth, freedom of information and protection of the individual.
- The most widely covered aspects in the codes are about journalists' accountability to the public, and to sources and referents. In some parts of the world, particularly in non-democratic and authoritarian states, emphasis is also placed on journalists' accountability to the State and employers.
- Linked to this is the importance of and protection of a journalist's integrity. It is, however, significant that emphasis is also placed on the public, sources and referents, in relation to protecting the integrity and status of the journalist. This means that the codes are designed not just for the selfish purpose of securing the narrow interests of journalists, but also for the broader purpose of serving public interest.

If one were to set out the most important principles in the existing European journalistic codes, they may summarised as follows. Responsible and professional journalism must be based on:

- truthfulness in gathering and reporting information;
- freedom of expression and comment, and the defence of these rights;
- equality, by not discriminating against anyone on the basis of his or her gender, race, ethnicity or religion, social class, profession, handicap, or any other personal characteristics;
- fairness, by using only direct means to gather information;
- respect for sources and referents, and their integrity, including respect for copyright laws;
- a duty not to divulge confidential sources;
- a duty not to prejudge the guilt of an accused and to publish the dismissal of charges against or acquittal of anyone about whom the newspaper previously had reported that charges had been filed or that a trial had commenced; and
- independence/integrity, by refusing bribes and resisting any form of outside influence on the work.

In many contexts, these principles are not necessarily respected or known in detail by practicing journalists. Thus, it is tempting to maintain that, in many circumstances, they only serve as a rhetorical device, as a set of principles brought to the fore when the press is under attack for overstepping ethical principles. However, it is important to uphold ethical standards as an ideal, even if it is one that journalists do not always live up to in their day-to-day practice of meeting deadlines, gathering the latest news, not having time to check sources properly, etc.

Codes of ethical conduct have been carefully elaborated on and adopted by representative professional bodies consisting of journalists, editors and publishers. They function as instruments of self-reflection by helping the practitioners to understand the nature of their work and relating their practice to broader moral and ethical values. They are constantly debated and revised, expressing a continual concern about ethical standards in the media. For example, most European codes are the result of revisions that have taken place since the second half of the 1980s, but mainly in the 1990s. They reflect not only the fundamental changes in Europe since 1989/1990, but also the developments in media and communication during the 1990s.

MECHANISMS OF SELF-REGULATION

Many European countries have press councils – Austria, Germany, the Netherlands, Norway, Sweden, and the UK, as does Australia. While there is no Canadian national press council, five of the provinces have their own councils, and four provinces have a regional council. In some countries (e.g. Canada, the USA and the UK), newspapers have appointed their own ombudsman, often journalism professors, to consider readers' complaints and make recommendations to the editors. In the UK, however, they seem to have only limited influence. The value of an effective press council is that it provides a process that is quicker and less expensive than a court hearing for resolving complaints against the press. However, some critics counter that press councils contribute little to protecting press freedom or countervailing individual interests (such as in privacy or reputation), given the weakness of their sanctions.

Press councils have authority to hear and decide on cases of individual complaints against the press.

Press councils have authority to hear and decide on cases of individual complaints against the press. A few also promote press freedom by contributing to public policy debates and making representations to their governments. In addition to a press council, Sweden has a press ombudsman, and the executive secretary of the

Australian Press Council serves in a role similar to that of an ombudsman. Both attempt to mediate disputes before they are submitted to the more formal procedures of the councils. National press councils were established in response to calls by the public for the statutory regulation of perceived journalistic excesses. Press councils are financed by their constituent press associations; most include public members who do not have a media background, and some are chaired by lawyers. The Swedish, Norwegian and Dutch press councils are among the most effective. All include non-press members, and the Swedish and Dutch councils have lawyers as chairs to improve the consistency of judgments, and to assist in promoting and clarifying standards through the development of 'councils' case law'.

Most press councils allow complaints to be filed only by people who are directly or indirectly mentioned or affected by a media report. However, the Norwegian Press Council authorises that the secretary-general of the Press Association (who is not a member of the Press Council) has the right to file complaints on his or her initiative. Most press councils hold hearings at which the parties may present evidence. The chief sanction is the obligation of an offending newspaper to publish any negative findings; the chief impetus for a newspaper to publish negative findings is the desire to remain a member of the association or council in good standing, and to impress on the public that it plays by the rules.

Independent media should be accountable, not to governments or political parties, but to their audiences ...

Most press councils try to discourage plaintiffs from taking their complaints to the courts because the complaints process then becomes redundant and the press will be inclined to disregard it. In Sweden, dissatisfied complainants occasionally file lawsuits, and courts occasionally support their judgments with arguments drawn from the council's opinion and ethical principles. The press is particularly unhappy when the results of a voluntary process are used against them in court, but in practice, the number of such cases is small. Press councils have worked reasonably well in keeping the number of lawsuits against the press low and in safeguarding press freedom. All have proved reasonably satisfactory to the press and to the public in safeguarding the privacy of individuals while permitting scrutiny and criticism of politicians and public officials.

The effectiveness of a press council in promoting responsible reportage while safeguarding essential press freedoms may be judged according to three main factors:

- the degree to which the ethical guidelines forming the basis of its decisions adequately balance the protection necessary for the press to perform its special functions, and various governmental and individual interests;

- the consistency and forcefulness with which the council applies ethical standards; and
- the degree to which newspapers comply with the council's decisions.

Probably the two most important factors accounting for the councils' success is that major and influential newspapers respect their decisions, and that the public have confidence in their decisions. Major newspapers tend to respect the councils' decisions where there are strong publishers' associations that actively support them. The public's respect appears to depend on whether the press actively complies with the council's decisions. This, combined with the participation of non-media members on the councils, contributes to their legitimacy with the general public and political interests.

The role of media ethics and the possibility of establishing media councils were hotly debated issues in southern Africa during the 1990s. These issues have been raised by the Media Institute of Southern Africa (MISA), which has held that journalism ethics is a very important component in advocating and sustaining free, diverse and independent media in southern Africa. MISA regards ethics as part of media accountability.

For the media to be believable, the public must know that journalists operate according to ethical codes and that they know what these codes imply. Furthermore, the codes must be enforceable; if they are not, they are meaningless. Independent media should be accountable, not to governments or political parties, but to their audiences – the reading, viewing and listening public.

MISA holds that the mechanism for establishing accountability lies in the setting up of voluntary media councils similar to those established in Europe, consisting of representatives of working journalists, editors and public representatives. MISA therefore supports the concept of voluntary media councils to adjudicate complaints based on accepted ethical codes for the media. There have been discussions in MISA about appointing a regional ombudsman for journalists. He or she would be a specialist in media ethics and media law, and fulfil various functions. One function would be to act as a special advisor to voluntary national media councils in the region, and another would be to act as a brake on governments in the region in relation to legal action. The ombudsman would meet with governments and try to persuade them to withdraw legal action in favour of other methods of arbitration. If a media council does not exist, the ombudsman would attempt to mediate the dispute between the government and the media institution concerned.

Having both media councils and a regional ombudsman for journalists might result in significant monetary savings for governments and their citizens, and contribute to the sustainability of independent media in the region, which at best have a fragile and precarious financial existence.

It should be a condition of all media council arbitrations that parties appearing before the council (both the plaintiff and the defendant) waive their rights to legal action. Thus, governments that choose to litigate instead of referring their complaints to the media council would be demonstrating vindictiveness towards the concept of free media. There is, however, quite a strong opinion being voiced, also within African media, that African journalists are so inexperienced, have such limited knowledge of ethical issues, and do not really care principally about press freedom, that media councils may make poor decisions and set dangerous precedents. In such a case, it may be better for journalists to appear before the courts, so that they themselves do not contribute to their own oppression.

Many governments in the SADC are sceptical about the establishment of voluntary media councils. The official position seems to be that such councils amount to creating a situation where journalists become a law unto themselves.

In some ways this view is correct, because the logic that underpins a voluntary media council is that it is an institution where the media and journalists are held responsible by their peers and by public representatives. They should operate in an open and transparent manner. What makes councils potentially powerful is that they are not dependent on outside influence; they are organs for the media. It is so easy to cry foul and allege violation of press freedom when the government or a politician criticises newspapers and journalists. However, it is not so easy to scorn such criticism when, hypothetically speaking, it comes from media peers, who share the same press freedom values.

While governments have been suspicious of the setting up of voluntary and independent councils, there have been several suggestions for the creation of official organs to ensure that the media upholds ethical standards (e.g. in Zambia and in Tanzania). These proposals have often consisted of members appointed by press organs, government and civil society.

What may be said in favour of such a system is that government approval gives the council a form of official legitimacy. However, it may be argued that this set up undermines independence. In this context, it may be worth noting that press organisations in Europe have in general been sceptical of institutionalising the media ombudsman as part of the legal system.

ETHICS AND PRACTICAL JOURNALISTIC WORK

NEWS CRITERIA

Many analyses of what constitutes news have concluded that there are some universal criteria. Events make news if they are unusual, unexpected or unpredictable. News is linked to the medium's production cycle. The news stories selected from the wire services of the world are dependent on media production schedules: whether for a daily newspaper, an hourly news bulletin on radio, or, in the era of around-the-clock television news, whether they break the repetitious cycle of stories by being sensational – for example, involving catastrophes, wars, hijackings, celebrities, etc.

Events become news if they involve well-known people or groups, places or countries; if they are close to home (literally and figuratively); if they are negative (e.g. accidents), or reach a certain volume (e.g. numbers injured or money involved). News can be seen as a form of culture, known as 'public knowledge', in that when the media offer the public an item of news, they confer upon it public legitimacy. The news media bring stories into a common public forum where a general audience can discuss them. News relates to, but is not the same as ideology; news is related to, but is not the same as information. News is produced by people who operate, often unwittingly, within a cultural system of meanings and patterns of discourse. News as a culture makes assumptions about what makes sense, the time and place in which we live, and what we should take seriously.

PUBLIC INTEREST V THE RIGHT TO PRIVACY

The role of the press in focusing on public figures and institutions – such as politicians, governments, State agencies, organisations and companies – is relatively clear when it comes to ethical considerations and relevance. The role of the press in relation to private individuals is ethically more complicated, and needs to be discussed and weighed constantly.

One of the functions of the press is to find out the truth in matters of public concern. This is paramount in the duty of the press to uncover cases of abuse. However, to maintain the principle of public concern may conflict with and disrupt the privacy of an individual, as making things public implies interrupting privacy. The line between what constitutes the private sphere and the public sphere is constantly debated, and changes with history and cultures. In general, the 'private' is the area over which individuals feel they have control. Claims to privacy imply the right to control access to one's personal domain, and it is something that most individuals want to protect. Some of the most vicious dictatorships that have existed have not respected the right to privacy. Violations of privacy in the form of censorship of letters, phone tapping, etc., are seen as infringements of citizens' and human rights. The right to privacy is safeguarded in Article 12 of the Universal Declaration of Human Rights of 1948, where it is stated:

> No one shall be subjected to arbitrary interference with his privacy, family, home or correspondence, nor to attacks upon his honour and reputation. Everyone has the right to the protection of the law against such interference or attacks.

The right to privacy and particularly the question of what constitutes honour and reputation are relevant to the complex issue of libel law and defamation. In many countries, law protects some areas of privacy. More important in this context are the ethical considerations that have to be observed when the press deals with issues of privacy. Ethical rules tend to vary, but there are some rules that are observed universally. To break these is seen as going against the accepted ethos of the media. One example is that the press should avoid naming rape victims, so that they are spared the additional pain of being publicly identified. Another, more contested issue, is that the press in many countries are reluctant to publish the names of people accused of crimes when the trial has not yet determined guilt. The reasoning behind this is that no one is guilty until proven guilty, and to cast suspicion on an innocent person is, in many ways, tantamount to a sentence. There have been cases where people who have been accused of crimes and later found innocent, but portrayed by the press as being guilty, have been awarded substantial compensation.

In some countries (e.g. Sweden and Norway), politicians have proposed that it should be illegal for the media to identify the accused in criminal cases until after the verdict has been passed, in order to protect the privacy of innocent people who might be involved in criminal proceedings. Such proposals have, however, been severely criticised by the press for reasons linked to the principle of openness in the judicial system and public trials. If, for example, the identity of the accused were kept secret, it would be more difficult for them to rally support. In countries where journalists are subject to ongoing government harassment and arrest, they would be disadvantaged if their colleagues could not report that they had been arrested.

Furthermore, secrecy would serve as blueprint for rumour mongering, and it is argued that only dictatorships wish to keep judicial proceedings secret. If such a law were passed, publishing photographs revealing police brutality would be against the law.

Questions of privacy are extremely complicated from an ethical point of view. What principally falls within the public interest, and what is principally a private matter? For example, if a newspaper reveals that a minister has had a foreign holiday paid for by an international company in return for contracts, it is clearly in the public interest that this matter be brought out in the open, as it is an example of abuse of office. It is a private matter whom the minister took with him on holiday, even if it might have been a piquant additional story. However, this story might be a public matter if the minister took along a mistress while campaigning for family values and was a fierce critic of all forms of moral slackness, castigating his public opponents for moral failure. This would reveal him as a political hypocrite, and publishing a story about his actions would be deemed to be in the public interest.

... the public has a right to be informed about matters that might affect its welfare.

One way of dealing with the problem of what constitutes a justifiable disruption of privacy is to say that the personal affairs of a public person are only newsworthy if they are relevant to another obviously newsworthy story. Do public figures have a diminished right to privacy? Should the fact that they have chosen to enter the public arena imply that they should be willing to suffer the consequences of embarrassing revelations? Many argue this point by referring to media practices in the USA, which may endanger the political process because many potentially able politicians will not risk having their own and their family's private lives publicly revealed. The argument goes that a media practice that is preoccupied with private details loses sight of what really ought to be in the public interest. A counter-argument is that the demand for privacy by public figures can be used to hide secret activities that are either illegal or blameworthy, and that the media have a justifiable interest in reporting these.

What constitutes public interest? Unfortunately, there is no doubt that the media make ambiguous use of the notion. Sometimes it is taken to mean, what is in the interests of the public to know, or what the public is interested in. The latter is frequently used to defend tabloid media with high sales. Since some sections of the media's public buy into any amount of gossip and scandal, the notion of public interest becomes whatever is newsworthy; and anything a newspaper wishes to print is, by definition, newsworthy. However, the public has a right to be informed about matters that might affect its welfare. This has to do with the notion of social responsibility and suggests that public interest has to do with what is of essential social importance, of benefit to society, and of public concern for reasons of political and economic decision-making.

Privacy can be disrupted in different ways, including the publication of embarrassing private facts, which, in principle, are of no public interest. Many reports of this kind involve dubious journalistic practices, which often constitute violation of someone's private space. For example, a journalist may enter a home uninvited or besiege someone's house. It may involve taking photographs using telephoto lenses or publishing information that places someone in a false light by reporting falsehoods and distortions. Many of these practices have been known to occur in the name of paparazzi journalism.

Three groups of people are frequently caught in the media limelight: politicians; 'public personalities' – celebrities who are created and maintained by the media, or have exploited the media to promote themselves; and those who are involuntarily thrust into the public eye. The last group is most in need of protection, yet least able to secure it.

Two other issues should be considered in this context. The first is the moral rights of subjects of photographs. Photographs of celebrities or public figures in their public roles may be fair game, but is it right to use images of ordinary people, particularly when they are caught up in extraordinary situations, such as war, terrorism, or other violence? This involves intrusion into grief in the aftermath of disasters or violent incidents, such as innocent victims of crime. Microphones are thrust in front of victims, who may be in a state of shock. Grieving relatives are asked how they feel. Executions are reported in gruesome detail, both in the USA and in Third World countries. Is it ethical for people to be shown dead, dying, or in distress, in poverty or suffering famine? Such images are very powerful and are the staple diet of what has been dubbed 'disaster journalism' particularly in Third World countries, but they are an intrusion of privacy.

Should there be strict guidelines for using such images, with provisions for consent by the subjects? The coverage of, for example, famine in Somalia or genocide in Rwanda raises serious ethical questions.

CONFLICT OF INTEREST

Journalists often find themselves in situations where they experience a conflict of interest; where there is a clash between what is professionally and ethically the right thing to do, and outside interests and pressures. A conflict of interest occurs in situations concerning economics, the use of favours to influence reporting, politics, and personal relationships.

Journalists who report on stock-market fluctuations illustrate the economic aspect of this form of conflict. They are often in a position to find out which shares are going to be mentioned in influential business columns, or they might write these themselves, and therefore have knowledge that could influence the value of the shares. If journalists share this information, and it is used to sell shares in advance of the rest of the market and make large profits, this is not only a blatant breach of ethics, but also illegal.

This is an extreme example, but in the day-to-day activities of ordinary reporters, they often encounter situations where it is difficult to decide what borders on unethical behaviour. This is particularly the case when journalists are offered gifts or favours. These may be innocent and not involve any promises. They may take the form of having a dinner paid for by a news source, or free trips paid for by a vested interest. Such trips may provide useful access to news stories – for example, where aid organisations arrange and pay for journalists to travel to projects or disaster areas. Whereas the objective is to focus interest on the need for aid, it may carry with it problems of conflicting interests for the journalists involved. Similarly, travel writers are often offered free trips to holiday destinations. In both cases the journalists might not have been able to undertake the assignment if expenses were not paid. Given this scenario, can the journalist write a balanced story? Can the journalist write critically? Many newspapers maintain a firm position about not accepting this kind of favour, as it is believed to jeopardise independent reporting.

Another question is whether journalists should be involved in public organisations and, particularly, in politics? By participating in the organisational life of a community, journalists keep in touch with the society they cover, and this may give them access to useful news sources. However, many maintain the position that journalists should not be part of the system they are assigned to cover.

Personal relationships can create a conflict of interest. Reporters are sons and daughters, wives and husbands; they also have friends. They belong to a community; they have identities and personal histories. They have experiences that involve close contacts, ranging from close personal relationships to business associates. Such relationships may create ethical problems. A journalist may be given highly sensitive information on the understanding that it is not to be published; he or she is 'taken into the know'. This means that the journalist has information that might be useful at a later date, or that provides useful background, but it also means that that journalist is bound in his or her reporting.

When there is a conflict of interest, the media lose credibility. It is often difficult to avoid such conflicts, but they should at least be acknowledged, so that the public can consider them; more than any other factor, news media and journalists need public credibility.

CONFIDENTIALITY OF SOURCES

Confidentiality is associated with many professions, including medical doctors, lawyers, priests, social workers, and accountants. But it is also central to journalistic ethics. In some countries, such as Sweden and Germany, a journalist's right to refuse to reveal the identity of a source is legally protected in the same way that the law safeguards a doctor's or a priest's right to confidentiality. Journalists may be asked to reveal their source of information, particularly when a newspaper has revealed corruption in high places, or has information on criminal activities. When the police want to know the source, the principle of keeping a source confidential is tested, particularly if the reporter has information the police believe they need to investigate a crime. Journalists generally feel that the police should develop their own sources, and resent becoming an arm of law enforcement.

The relationship between a source and a journalist is a special one. Journalists believe in source confidentiality for several reasons, and it is difficult to underestimate the importance for a journalist to obtain information in confidence from a source and then protect the confidentiality of that source. The crucial ethical issue is whether anonymity should be promised in the first place, because to do so may conflict with other demands. There are times when journalists believe that they will not get the information unless confidentiality can be promised, and thus the readers would not be informed about matters of public interest. The principle of confidentiality imposes a duty on the journalist to withhold the names of sources from third parties.

So far, it has been assumed that the reporter's privilege of keeping confidence is a good thing. But there is the issue of whether a news organisation should publish secret or confidential information provided by a source. In principle, sources should be made known; readers may only able to judge the value of the information provided if they are able to evaluate its source. Confidentiality deprives the audience of the opportunity to decide for itself how much faith to place on the information. In other words, the names of the sources are an important part of the story.

An illustration of the problems surrounding confidentiality is the case where, in October 1992, the editor and a journalist of the Zimbabwean weekly *Financial Gazette* were called before a parliamentary committee and ordered to reveal the source of a leak from the committee investigating corruption by senior officials. Parliament appointed a committee on privileges to consider whether further action should be taken against the journalists and the two members of the committee responsible for the leak. The regulation used to back this case was the Privileges, Immunities and Power of Parliament Act, which is linked to the Official Secrets Act. Both pieces of legislation date back to the UDI-period[28] and have parallels to British practice during the Thatcher era, which was a combination of relatively authoritarian State control in terms of the publication of so-called 'State secrets', and a government that was a proponent of a radical form of economic liberalism. The British practices are very different from the American situation, where it is very difficult for the authorities to use reason for official secrets as an argument against media coverage. There is, of course, the problem of principle, when the institution that ideally should defend the citizens' right to information – parliament – actually curtails it. In the case of the *Financial Gazette*, the editor maintained that:

> ... contrary to what was reported, (...) we did not reveal the source of our stories. Instead one of the sources decided to confess to the chairman of the committee, and was then compelled to make his confession to the entire committee.[29]

Only then did the editor acknowledge his source. This case has several interesting aspects pertaining to the freedom and independence of the media. The first is the problem of a parliament that, in this case, can be interpreted as pressurising the press and forcing its subservience to the State. The second concerns the principle of protecting sources, which is imperative for a press that is accountable to the public, and for the safety of those individuals who expose malpractices through the media. Cases involving journalists and editors defending their rights to safeguard sources have been among the most important in the history of the free press, and particularly in the history of the Zimbabwean press. In 1933, the then editor of *The Bulawayo Chronicle*, Sydney Veats, was imprisoned for refusing to reveal a source. His stance received wide support.[30]

The way in which the editor of the *Financial Gazette* dealt with the case has some unfortunate aspects. Even when the Members of Parliament had come forward, he should not have acknowledged them as his sources, as it jeopardised the principle of absolute confidentiality of sources. Secondly, as Professor Jonathan Moyo points out:

> ... the surrender was unfortunate because Parliament should have been challenged. In a constitutional democracy committed to transparency

and accountability in the formulation of public policy, it is neither reasonable nor justifiable to have select committees meet behind closed doors and sit as courts. The public have a right to know.

The Privileges Act has several unconstitutional aspects and they should be taken up by constitutional lawyers and human rights groups. The Act fails to honour the distinction between parliamentary democracy and constitutional democracy.[31]

NEWSGATHERING, INVESTIGATION AND CHECKING SOURCES

One of the greatest challenges of investigative journalism lies in the roles ethics play in relation to the methods used to obtain news stories. It not only concerns methods of gathering information, but also the way in which the story is presented. It concerns the use of deception, economy of truth, and even direct lying as a way of obtaining information. Undercover reporting is a common practice, which obviously entails deception, as does the use of hidden cameras in television-news reportage. Is this justifiable? Many journalists feel that forms of deceit are the only way to expose those who would prefer to remain un-exposed, and that they are necessary and acceptable working procedures for a vigorous, strong press. This is particularly the case in societies where access to information is seriously hampered by stringent secrecy acts, and there exists no principle of the public's right to information. Ethical codes in several countries allow subterfuge 'in the public interest'. As a defence for such practices, it is often argued that journalists are representatives of the public, and deception in the name of the public interest is sometimes necessary to uncover corruption, social ills and a wide range of dubious activities. One may accept unethical practices if the result is that social ethics are upheld; that the end justifies the means. However, there is every reason to debate this because the means sometimes becomes the end, with the losers being ethical journalism and the credibility of the news media.

A distinction may be drawn between active and passive deception. It is passive when a person does not reveal his or her true identity; for example, a restaurant critic seems to be justified in withholding his or her identity. But what about pretending to be someone else, or having a different profession or identity to obtain information and a story? This is active deception, amounting to a lie. The famous German journalist, Gunther Walraff, used such tactics to gather information for several well-known critical books on reportage revealing, for example, abuses of power and activities of right-wing organisations. One of his most controversial exploits was when he managed, using a false name and credentials, to get a job with the German right-wing populist and extremely popular scandal newspaper *Bild Zeitung*. (It is not printed in tabloid format, but its journalistic content is tabloid.) He used the information he gathered while working at the newspaper to expose, what he regarded as, unethical journalistic methods of his colleagues and the press ideology that ruled *Bild Zeitung*. Walraff used investigative techniques that many would question, but it was the only way he could gather proof of how *Bild Zeitung* broke with ethical reporting in its journalistic practice. But what happens in cases where journalists break the law to illustrate the malfunctioning of institutions?

One must remember that journalists or newspapers that use lying or deception become involved in a web of deceit that pervades the newsgathering process. Taking shortcuts in one area can easily lead to shortcuts in others (the truth of the facts reported). Secondly, journalists may take part in practices they criticise in others, notably government, which they would protest against if they were carried out on themselves, as newspaper organisations or individuals. There is a tendency for journalists to argue that, if the crime or malpractice exposed is worse than the deception required in exposing it, then it is justified. This will nearly always be the case, especially if journalistic deception is common. Possibly the most consistent ethical attitude is to be very careful about using any form of deceit or subterfuge, and to only resort to such techniques when all alternative approaches have failed, and when the story is of extreme public interest.

Sometimes the claim of confidentiality of sources may be a smoke-screen for shoddy journalistic work in checking and double-checking sources. News sources supply information for a variety of motives, not all of which are praiseworthy. They may be providing information out of self-interest or for revenge. How are journalists to know whether this information has been altered, edited or selected out of context? Whose interest are they serving? There is the very real danger that journalists, and through them, the public, can be deceived by this use of confidentiality. In several countries, the government uses a system of informal, unattributed briefings to the press, known as the 'lobby system'. This has allowed governments and individual politicians to manipulate news to the point of 'disinformation'. When journalists are presented with secret information about important issues, they become, in a very real sense, agents for the furtive source. This practice is becoming increasingly widespread beyond politics, in business, in public relations, where 'spin-doctors' and information bureaus, lobbyists and agents try to influence media coverage by taking journalists into their confidence and feeding them information that, in many cases, may be doubtful, if not deceitful.

With the development of the Internet, the question of checking sources has reached a new level. So many stories circulate on the web that are of dubious quality, that to uncritically make use of them seriously jeopardises the trustworthiness of the news media. There have also been cases of journalists fabricating Internet sources when both editors and the public were taken in by the scam.

It is not in the long-term interest of good journalism to connive in such practices. The extensive use of unattributed sources promotes distrust and even cynicism towards reported stories. Journalists should not let their desire to obtain information undermine the long-term credibility of the information they present to the public. Of even greater importance is that good journalistic ethics implies a principled openness in public discourse. Good reporting and democratic journalism challenges secrecy. The news media should therefore avoid secrecy as much as possible and revert to it only in very special cases.

OBJECTIVITY, IMPARTIALITY AND TRUTH

There is a widespread assumption that journalists should aim to be impartial and objective. This is believed by many critics to be impossible. Also, the press, and to an increasing extent radio and television, use columnists and commentators who are opinionated, who have a point of view to put over.

News reporters are often far from being distanced, neutral observers. Journalists are implicated in the events on which they are reporting; they cannot and should not avoid making and reporting evaluative judgements about them. This may be interpreted as an argument against objectivity, but it is not, for the question here is: What is implied by journalistic objectivity? Rather than implying lack of engagement, it involves arriving at the appropriate report after interpreting and evaluating a state of affairs. Impartiality, unlike neutrality, does not preclude evaluative judgements.

Good journalism should not just describe how and why an event happened, but attempt to show its true nature. For example, in the case of a war massacre, it is most important to highlight the truly evil and horrific nature of what has been perpetrated. Objectivity can then be achieved rationally, applying the basic principles of interpretation and evaluation.

Journalists have a duty to strive for impartiality, and thus objectivity, but this is not the same as losing sight of the importance of maintaining values. Possessing values does not prevent one from seeing and telling the truth. If news is being written, the journalist must base his or her reporting on values, because news is a quasi-evaluative concept that renders and interprets what has taken place.

The culture of one form of journalism often presumes that impartiality requires journalists to focus upon the failings and possible hidden motives of public characters. Such issues are pertinent when considering the interrelationships of journalism and politics. In the party politics of the USA and Europe, and with the development of multiparty systems in many other parts of the world, the emerging network of political advisors develop techniques to get the most favourable 'spin' on a story for their party. This may be an incentive to look for hidden motives. The press is increasingly faced with the practices of press agents or 'spin doctors', who operate mostly in politics and negotiate access to the politicians and decision-makers they represent. They are therefore in a position to set the conditions under which their employer will appear on television – for example, who the interviewer will be, what questions are off-limits, who else will appear on the programme, etc. This may lead to a confrontational style of political journalism marked by a degree of cynicism, which, again, may lead to contempt of politicians and politics. These arguments have been put forward particularly in Europe, where a decline in voter participation has been blamed on, amongst other factors, cynical political reporting. However, it has been argued that journalists need to maintain a sceptical approach, to combat politicians' attempts to control the news agenda in ways that serve their interests, and are often distinct from the public's.

The press is increasingly faced with the practices of press agents or 'spin doctors', who operate mostly in politics and negotiate access to the politicians and decision-makers they represent.

Impartiality, objectivity and the public interest are difficult terms and principles to realise. In the vast number of articles and books written during and after the Gulf War, many critical journalists and media scholars point out that Western media distorted the war and became a conduit for an American public relations exercise. They forgot about checking sources and about being critical of where the material they used came from, and also forgot to ask whose interests were served by reporting the war in the way they did. Many of those who have analysed the media coverage of the Gulf War, maintain that the media played a distorting role in constructing the world audience's understanding of the war.

Particularly in war and conflict reporting, there is every reason to question whether the media report the truth or only part of the truth. However, to what extent can the whole truth be told? The international media coverage of the 'war against terrorism' in 2001, and the war in

Afghanistan, which according to *The International Herald Tribune* of 22 October 2001, is the most media-controlled war in modern history, illustrates this problem very well.

In early modern European thinking, freedom of expression (the right to freely voice opinions and discuss conflicting ideas) would lead to an understanding of what was true. Freedom of speech was a prerequisite to finding truth. This way of thinking developed into the view that the role of the media is to inform citizens, and provide them with correct, truthful information, in order for them to make informed decisions. In this context the media primarily deal with news and informational material. We are not dealing with media that provide fiction.

It has become a commonplace pronouncement that comment is free, facts are sacred, and that the press has an obligation to print the truth. But truth is a tricky concept, even if most ethical codes begin with the journalist's duty to tell the truth under all conditions. This applies not only to the journalist's actual reports, but also to the methods used to gather news. Immediately we run into the problem of the use of subterfuge, for not telling the truth may, in some situations, be justified in order to gain important information.

It has been suggested that, in the day-to-day activities of a news organisation, what is newsworthy is more important than noble assertions about truth. Many commentators on media practices have maintained that news reporting and truth seeking may have different purposes, and that it is only possible to combine truth and news when one reports facts, such as election results, or the outcome of sports events. When the topic of the report is in dispute, objective truth should not be expected of the news media, if such a thing exists.

What constitutes truth is a very complex philosophical question. Is truth-telling necessary to society? It is widely accepted that it is since lack of integrity in human communications undermines the autonomy of the individual. Similarly, trust is based on truthful communication, and lying and deception undermine the foundations of society. However, journalists are not just supposed to be telling the truth, but to be finding it out; they need to do more than achieve truthfulness. One can ask journalists how much care they have taken to find out the truth? How much care have they taken to be truthful? We might also ask: Is there an attempt to be fair, to be balanced, to avoid bias? The last question acknowledges that the whole truth is elusive and sometimes, perhaps always, impossible. Questions such as these are at the heart of ethical practices in journalism.

The desire of the press to report the truth is frequently opposed by those who may have reason to fear the truth, including governments. Clearly, reporting the truth is often harmful to others. When it comes to uncovering malpractice in public office, bringing the truth out into the open may harm certain highly placed people, but this is relatively unproblematic from an ethical perspective. The issue of telling the truth, using euphemisms, or shying away from the truth, may involve issues that morally are much more difficult.

For example, the press is often discreet in obituaries about the cause of death if it was attributed AIDS. In the USA and in Europe, this practice is now changing. Originally, it was thought using phrases like 'after a long illness' would spare the family's feelings. However, by not admitting that people died of AIDS, this practice of non-reporting confirmed people's prejudices about the disease. Further, if a person dies young and no reason is given for his or her cause of death, this in itself leads to speculation.

Three criteria for truth in news reporting have been suggested. The first is accuracy; the facts should be based on solid evidence. Secondly, a news story should promote understanding. The story should contain as much relevant information as is available and essential to provide the average reader or viewer with some understanding of the facts and the context of the facts. Thirdly, reporting should be fair and balanced. All three criteria have problematic aspects.

ACCURACY

Reported stories should be accurate; the facts presented in a report should be based on solid evidence. However, accuracy may be threatened by the competitive practices of journalism. Where speed is of the essence, information may be broadcast before it has been verified. Some journalists are lazy or casual about accuracy. Once an inaccuracy becomes news, it is often repeated and magnified, if journalists' research does not go further than previous newspaper stories. Given a newsworthy story, there is little temptation for further research that might show the story to be false – leaving the journalist with a space to fill. Failure to check information carefully may not only lead to the newspaper receiving hoaxes, but also harm innocent people. This is particularly serious, because newspapers are reluctant to publish corrections and, if the story appears in many newspapers, it automatically receives increased authenticity.

The blending of fact and fiction in television docudramas raises important ethical issues.

A specific issue raised by the requirement of accuracy is whether it is permissible to stage or restage events. This applies particularly to photographs and film or video material. One of the most trivial practices on television news is where reporters and anchors introduce interviews over footage of the interviewee walking, or on the telephone, or reading a document – all activities staged for the camera. When there is no real-life footage, it is a common practice in television news to create mini docudramas, which are presented as if they are real.

The blending of fact and fiction in television docudramas raises important ethical issues. Not only have they become a popular entertainment format, they are also increasingly used to dramatise documentary and reality television programmes. Television uses various formats, and the line between fact and fiction is often blurred. 'Reconstructions' are enactments of confidential public events but are subject to a strong element of creation in that a script has to be written. That actors are used implies distortion of fact. This stricture also applies to the format of reality television, which tends to be the re-enactment of crimes or rescue attempts, and the transmission of tapes from the real event – often shot by amateurs, or by roving reporters following the heels and wheels of police patrols, ambulances and fire engines. This raises several problems. One would be the claim, implicit or explicit, that the events shown happened in that way. The second is that the portrayal of dramatic events, such as murders, police raids, suicides, violent family quarrels, social problems, illness – all of which are broadcast on reality television shows – represent invasion of privacy, and often go against what is generally regarded as being in good taste, however dramatic they may be.

Photographs, because of their high degree of selectivity and what might be termed their credibility in showing reality, can easily create a misleading impression. These problems have been exacerbated by developments in digital technology and computer graphics. It is now easy to alter photographs or create photographs that have no link to reality; images can be created of events that have not happened. Should altering a photograph be treated as a deliberate inaccuracy, with the intention to mislead?

Many news reports include quotations. These should be accurate, but is it wrong for a reporter to correct faulty grammar? Indirect quotes or paraphrases could be used, but journalists are reluctant to relinquish the vividness of direct quotation. Radio and television interviews can be manipulated through editing. For example, an answer to one question may be edited to appear to be the answer to another and this could give the listener or viewer quite a different perspective about what was said.

UNDERSTANDING

Simply observing accuracy in an article or report might be described as a minimal virtue. The facts reported may be correct, but they could still give a poor picture of what has occurred. However, not all facts about an event can be reported; the space for a newspaper report, for instance, is limited. In this sense, to print the whole truth is impossible, but it is a golden rule that a diligent journalist must provide an account that promotes understanding, and is based on knowledge of the situation that is being reported. In many situations, this principle is not adhered to, and the author has at times maintained that journalists often compensate for poor knowledge with 'chutzpah' (a Yiddish word for impudence). Consider this example: A politician gives a speech in which he makes claims about a serious issue that a reporter believes may be false.

Does the journalist do his or her job properly if only the speaker is quoted accurately, and the assertions are left unverified? To simply quote the speaker involves less work, and will not bring the journalist into conflict with the politician. However, it is a breach of the public's trust when a newspaper publishes a report that is not based on a full understanding of the situation. Unfortunately, this kind of reporting is common. The late Zimbabwean journalist Willie Musarurwa called it 'minister and sunshine journalism', based on the formula: 'The sun was shining, and the minister said the following...'.

It is not always enough to provide an accurate record of the facts. Whereas journalists often have to provide background information or context, some media are better at doing this than others. It is perhaps a limitation of television news that it is all foreground; the immediacy of the pictures precludes sober analysis. Very little is conveyed in thirty minutes of television compared to what can be read in that time. This is not to assume that media more capable of analysis always provide it. Newspapers vary greatly in how much effort they put into promoting understanding, but a common critique of journalism is that it is about events, rather than about explaining processes.

Some journalists are too ready to accept and use conventional explanations, albeit unconsciously. Reality is translated into stereotypes, including stereotypical stories and explanations. Uncritical news reporting is often anchored in 'what everybody knows', the use of simplistic analogies, based on conventional explanations, legitimacies and evaluations of social phenomena that have been incorporated into journalism's stock of knowledge. As conventional wisdoms, they enable the journalist to make sense of the world and enable him or her to produce public accounts that are acceptable to editors, readers and sources.

Stereotyping in the media is widespread. This is problematic in that stereotypes are an extremely narrow way of viewing the world. They are a tool for communicating with a mass audience and appeal to prejudices. Stereotyping exploits the fact that we do need some categories, some classification of the world, but it weights the differences between cultures, social groups and individuals, and commonly affects racial minorities, the elderly, the handicapped and women, Examples of stereotyping include the general lack of understanding by Western media of the Third World: Africa is usually seen only in terms of war and famine, and Islam usually means fundamentalism.

An example of reverse stereotyping was included in a report by Africa-correspondent for the Norwegian Broadcasting Corporation, Tomm Kristiansen. In the early 1990s, when the wars in then Yugoslavia were raging, he took a television crew to Harare Gardens, Zimbabwe, and asked people what they thought of Europe and whether they would like to live there. In general, the answers he received fell into following three categories:

- Europe is cold;
- there is growing racism in Europe, particularly directed at people from Africa; and
- there are strong tendencies for European countries and nations to split up, and there are many ethnic wars.

Consequently, most of the people he interviewed would not like to live in Europe, even if they had complaints about the situation in Zimbabwe.

A contrasting reportage is one that all of us have seen repeatedly in one form or another. It consists of pictures of, for example, a white nurse holding a starving black child in her arms, trying to feed it, while she is surrounded by women and children desperately waiting to be fed, to be helped, to receive what may keep them alive for one more day. With a tired smile, she turns to the camera and appeals for more support. The reporter then enters the picture and gives a harrowing description of the suffering, interspersed by images of death, famine, war, and more death. The white aid worker and the white reporter are active, the black victims are passive; they are objects of charity and of journalism.

There seems to be a structural synergy between violence and the activities of relief agencies, between campaigns for humanitarian international aid and the images popular international media offer of Africa. Human suffering and violence are good for the media; they are dramatic.

Paradoxically it serves, particularly when it appears on television, as reassurance for northern audiences that, despite all the instability and suffering that exists in the rest of the world, life at home is relatively safe and stable. News reports of human-made and natural disasters and catastrophes become part of a daily ritual, where the differences between us and the others who live and die in such terrible circumstances, are confirmed.

To the public, Western relief workers attending to Third World disasters are sometimes portrayed as symbols of the fundamental decency of international aid and the work done by international non-governmental organisations (NGOs).

Press and television reports depict international relief workers as good Samaritans, as modern-day saints who know what they are doing and the areas in which they work. It is the relief workers who receive coverage and not the local people who do most of the menial work, like burying the dead, disinfecting mass graves, and who have first-hand experience of the suffering. They are portrayed as sufferers and the passive recipients of charity.

[The] symbiotic relationship between the world media and international aid organisations seriously threatens the principle of independent journalism ...

Aid agencies respond to disasters with media appeals for help. These appeals are linked to reporters visiting the disaster areas and filing reports about the suffering. Often journalists' only way into disaster areas is via aid organisations. They travel on their planes, in their convoys, and with their officials as guides and primary sources. The reporters get powerful stories and dramatic pictures, while the NGOs get their message about the suffering to millions of viewers and readers, which generates millions of dollars for their operations. This symbiotic relationship between the world media and international aid organisations seriously threatens the principle of independent journalism, and is a critical challenge to fundamental journalistic ethics. Journalists accompanying relief agencies sometimes inadvertently, or, although they will never confess to this, purposefully give a favourable picture of the work performed by the agencies. These reports are again used by the NGOs in their fund-raising activities and in justifying their work to controlling authorities.

In situations like these, journalists appear to forget the basics of their trade, such as questioning the partiality of their sources and securing the views of more than one informant. The political judgements of relief agency workers are often coloured by one particular perspective, but they are quoted as a true and objective voice. They are asked to comment on situations in which they are central players and are often allied to one of the sides involved in the crises. Their judgements are seldom questioned or placed in perspective by reporters bringing in other sources. Wittingly or unwittingly the aid workers, but more seriously the media, serve as a propaganda apparatus on behalf of authorities and aid agencies, and not as a critical and analytical institution. The reasons for these uncritical attitudes are complex, but one counts more than others – that disaster journalism is a form of action reporting related to war reporting. The aim is to get the story shown as it happens, in its most graphic horror, which implies that analytical questions are not asked.

What is practised is a form of parachute journalism. Reporters are literally dropped in the midst of suffering, and then lifted out with a story that has a strong human emphasis and powerful emotional appeal, but often does not say anything about the situation's background. Who are the players? Who is responsible?

In all disasters, even those caused by nature, both politics and the business of aid is involved. More often than not, disasters are the result of political choice. For example, it was only after the horrors in Rwanda, Somalia and Ethiopia had been reported in the world media, that the background was revealed and analysed. Rarely did the journalists covering the disasters tell this story. They were analysed by academics and a few reporters who, for years, had specialised in reporting on news in Africa. The majority of Western journalists covering the African crises know too little, and rely on each other and on what the aid workers and northern diplomats tell them, rather than on the people who live and die in African societies.

One of the most problematic aspects of disaster relief, particularly in war and conflict situations, is that aid workers are often dependent on officials and soldiers in the countries in which they work. While this may be an obstacle to the efficiency of relief campaigns, it is beyond the scope of this analysis. However, it implies the possibility of aid organisations having to enter into alliances with non-humanitarian forces to deliver aid.

In an attempt to deal with such contradictions, NGOs often downplay the problematics of the crises and conflicts, by making them more moralistic and clear-cut than they really are. Simultaneously, they allow visiting journalists to be taken in by the very same authorities on which the relief agencies depend. Thus, they prevent investigation of the human rights abuses perpetuated by the military authorities with which the aid agencies are forced to cooperate.

The mainstream popular media rarely ask questions about the political agendas behind the conflicts attended by aid organisations. Uncomfortable issues, such as how the aid may be hijacked or even given to soldiers, or how the struggle may be prolonged by humanitarian aid, are seen as confusing the public and compromising the dominant image of the relief organisations. These questions are often left to the minority media.[32]

FAIRNESS AND BIAS

The issues referred to above are closely related to the question of bias in the media. There is a long list of terms signifying ideals in this context, such as 'fair' and 'balanced' reporting; stories should be 'without bias'; they should be 'impartial'. To ask for fairness and balance is to ask that evaluative language be avoided, that the material should not be slanted. The history of newspapers does not present much evidence of fairness and impartiality. There appears to have been two major influences in raising it as a journalistic value: broadcasting and the rise of press agencies. In particular, the ethical values of the BBC's news services impose obligations of impartiality, fairness and balance. The major international press agencies introduced a second factor. They promoted the idea of impartiality as a valued journalistic objective. Because they supplied the same news to consumers whose individual circumstances varied, they constructed a product that was at once standard and flexible. The standard nature of the product also helped to bring about the substantial measure of uniformity in professional theory and practice, far beyond the confines of their initial markets.

General criticisms of notions of fairness and balance are that they are limited virtues, take the middle line, and thus exclude views that are more controversial. How fair and balanced can journalists be? Is it possible to report an event or series of events in a way that does not reflect the reporter's attitudes about the events and the people involved?

The news media of a particular society – both press and broadcasting – tend to construct accounts of events that are structured and framed by the dominant values and interests of that society, and to marginalise (if not exclude) alternative accounts. It would be very surprising if the media of a society did not have the same criteria of importance and did not make the same value judgements as that of the society in which they exist. However, which of society's value judgments, and which group's values and opinions dominate the media? Selection involves considering the structure, ownership and management of media organisations; the social backgrounds, career patterns and attitudes of professional communicators; patterns of interaction between communicators and other related occupational groups; and the influence of prevailing cultural values.

The media must be understood in relation to the characteristic mode of production in society, as functional sustainers of the 'corporate economy'. The media portray a limited view of the world – generally one subscribed to by society's privileged classes. It is the dominant set of ideas and views, and interests in accordance with these, that are mainly represented in the media. The media are ideological, carrying a world-view that structures the world and explains it to the audience. Some views are rendered acceptable, normal or commonsense; others are marginalised. In situations of social and political conflict and strife, there seems to be a situation where dominant media, linked to the power structures in society, struggle to maintain hegemony, while oppositional media, often grounded in varying social groupings, attempt to establish a counter-hegemony. Much of the struggle between the 'official media' and the 'independent media' in Africa in the 1990s may be interpreted from such a perspective.

ETHICS AND POLITICS

All issues subject to discussion and varying interpretation are based on individual and cultural backgrounds. Ultimately, media ethics deals with questions of taste, decency and quality, for which there are no watertight rules.

Among the issues pertaining to what is regarded as decent in some cultures, for example, is the discussion and depiction of sexual material. The most heated debate about this issue concerns pornography. Another area of contention is blasphemy, which reached global prominence with the publication of Salman Rushdie's novel *Satanic Verses*, which was regarded by many Muslims as insulting, and resulted in Ayatollah Khomeini issuing a *fatwa* (religious decree) against the novelist and his publishers. In this instance, there was a clear conflict between the principle of freedom of expression and the sacredness of religion.

Another area where decency plays an important role is that of violence, over which there have been heated discussions for at least two reasons. One is that many see violence, particularly on film, video and television, as leading to more violence, particularly among young people. In other words, to show violence on screen can have direct harmful social effects. The second concern is the visual depiction of victims of acts of violence and catastrophes. This is not only seen as an invasion of the privacy of the victims and their relatives, but also as being in poor taste, because such images appeal to sensationalism and voyeurism. In this context, images related to words also enter the debate. Photographs may be so graphic that they shock in a way that a written report about the same event would not. Publishing visual material related to murder, accidents and suicides in particular, often goes against what is commonly regarded as decency. It is in situations such as these that newsworthiness competes with the ethical sensibilities of the audience.

These challenges raise ethical problems, not only in the more traditional media, but also in others; some of these problems are particular to the world of digital and convergent media. One may illustrate this by questioning the controls and regulations over cable and satellite channels. In principle, people expect to see television programmes similar to those broadcast on ordinary 'terrestrial' channels. One of the most discussed aspects is that of morals and control over sexually explicit programming on satellite channels. On the one side, there is the paternalistic or authoritarian view that the viewing of pornography on cable and satellite channels must be controlled. On the other side, there is the libertarian attitude that, since channels are voluntarily subscribed to by mature adults, they should be free to watch what they want. They pay for the service and are fully aware of the content.

In most countries with a widespread and evolved system of cable and satellite channels, these channels have fewer regulations than the terrestrial channels, but must still adhere to some form of programme code. The wider problem is that satellite television cuts across national borders and therefore differing views on taste and decency issues. This is even more apparent when one considers the Internet, which can make available pornography, racist propaganda, the formula for crack cocaine, details of women for sale in Thailand and the Philippines, and how to make bombs. Most of what is available on the Internet is available in print form or in other media somewhere in the world. It is clear that it is not necessarily the material itself that is always the problem, but its availability in the home, its ease of access. The additional problem of the Internet is locating the source. It could be very difficult to track the source of offending or illegal material according to the laws of one country, when the source is in a foreign country with different and more liberal laws. Should an on-line service be treated as a common carrier (like a telephone company that cannot be held responsible for what people say) or should it be treated as a publisher (that can be held responsible)?

The dual role of the media has been, and will be in the future, to both inform and to entertain.

Quality can be applied in any area of the media, but internationally, the focus has been on the press and television. Conflict between the quality press and tabloid journalism is pronounced, and similarly between quality and 'trash' television. In both media, quality is threatened by the pursuit of profit, or the pursuit of large audiences. There is, however, an underlying, tacit understanding in this debate that quality refers to the taste commonly associated with Western high culture and not popular culture.

The debate focuses on whether a free market will automatically deliver quality as demanded by the consumer, or whether the pursuit of the highest ratings and readership at the lowest cost (the lowest common denominator) will inevitably erode quality standards. Some general questions are worth asking. Is there a natural conflict between high culture, which is, almost by definition, minority culture, and the mass media? Does the mass media have their own quality standards? What makes good television? What makes a good newspaper? Even if everyone agrees that soap operas are not 'quality' television, they still raise questions of quality. What makes one soap opera better than another? It has also been argued that quality is not really an issue, that it is just a legitimation of old hierarchies of judgement – a concept drained of meaning through years of abuse by those in power.

The debate about quality in the media tends to focus on the issue of entertainment. The question is whether the media has an obligation to elevate tastes or whether providing escapist fare is sufficient. The argument against escapism is that it may distance people from important social issues, and direct them from useful social participation and action. The diversion from real life can lead to individual and group apathy, and to lower cultural standards and popular tastes. Must all material produced for a mass audience have at least some social worth? The dual role of the media has been, and will be in the future, to both inform and to entertain.

NOTES

1 MacDonald, Barrie and Petheram, Michel. (1998) *Keyguide to Information Sources in Media Ethics.* London, Washington: Mansell.

2 *European Journal of Communication.* Vol. 12, No. 4, December 1997.

3 Belsey, Andrew and Chadwick, Ruth (eds). (1992) *Ethical Issues in Journalism and the Media.* London, New York: Routledge.

4 Kieran, Matthew (ed). (1998) *Media Ethics.* London, New York: Routledge.

5 Ekström, Mats and Norhstedt, Stig Arne. (1996) *Journalistikens etiska problem.* Stockholm: RabTn Prisma, Svenska Journalis-förbundet.

6 Wilson, John. (1996) *Understanding Journalism. A Guide to Issues.* London, New York: Routledge.

7 'Ethics' comes from the Greek *ethos,* which refers to the study of the principles that ought to underline behaviour. Accordingly, 'ethics' refers to the basic principles of behaviour and to the related discipline of good or bad human conduct. It is often referred to in the same context as morals (from Latin *mores,* customary behaviour). The etymology of 'ethical' and 'moral' might explain why no systematic way of distinguishing these terms has emerged. The British philosopher Alasdair MacIntyre points out that moral is the descendent of the Latin word *moralis.* However, *moralis* was a term coined by the ancient Roman philosopher Cicero, to translate the Ancient Greek word *eetikos.* Both terms broadly meant 'pertaining to character'. English renderings of these terms have been associated with matters other than character, but no clear, consistent patterns of difference between moral and ethical seem to have developed.

8 Some of the points in this overview have been taken from arguments used in Jaksa, James and Pritchard, Michael S. (1993) *Communication Ethics. Methods of Analysis.* Belmont, California: Wadsworth.

9 Lucie-Smith, Edward. (1997) 'Bodies of Evidence' in *Index on Censorship No. 6, 1997.* London

10 Siebert, Fred S., Peterson, Theodore and Schramm, Wilbur. (1956) *Four Theories of the Press.* Urbana: Illinois University Press.

11 McQuail, Denis. (1987) *Mass Communication Theory. An Introduction.* London: Sage

12 Williams, Raymond. (1962, 1968) *Communications.* Harmondsworth: Penguin.

13 Murdock, Graham. (1992) 'Citizens, Consumers and Public Culture' in Skovmand, Michael and Schroeder, Kim Christian. (1992) *Media*

Cultures. Reappraising Transnational Media. London, New York: Routledge

14 *See* Anderson, Benedict. (1983 and later) *Imagined Communities. Reflections on the Origin and Spread of Nationalism.* London: Verso.

15 Some of the following points are from McQuail, Denis. (1997) 'Accountability of Media to Society. Principles and Means' in *European Journal of Communication.* Vol. 12, No. 4, December 1997.

16 To illustrate... In a discussion about news agendas in Africa, an Angolan journalist from Angolan TV once told the author that, whereas terrible massacres had taken place in the civil war in the country, the top news story on Angolan TV news, with footage from CNN, was of the conflict in Bosnia. The Angolan terror only received minor coverage.

17 On the implications of the new communication ideology of optimism and abundance, John Keane has made some cautious remarks linked to the global communication gap. He writes:

'Abundance might indeed be said to be the ideology of the new computer-linked electronic communications networks. (...) One of the earliest intellectual versions of the same ideology was expressed in Ithiel de Sola Pool's *Technologies of Freedom*: "There is nothing about spectrum technology that today mandates bureaucratic control of what is transmitted ... There need be no scarcity of capacity or access." John Perry Barlow repeats the point in *Declaration of the Independence of Cyberspace*, that computer-linked networks "are creating a world that all may enter without privilege or prejudice accorded by race, economic power, military force, or station of birth". Elsewhere, Barlow claims that the advent of cyberspace heralds nothing less than "a new social space, global and antisovereign, within which anybody, anywhere, can express to the rest of humanity whatever he or she believes without fear. There is in these new media a foreshadowing of the intellectual and economic liberty that might undo all the authoritarian powers on earth."

'Caution should be exercised when pondering these claims, not least because the new age of developing communicative abundance is unstable, even self-contradictory. Just as the growth of material abundance fails to produce what Marcuse called "happy consciousness", so communicative abundance contains new contradictions and produces new conflicts. Confusions and disagreements about who gets what, when, and how actually multiply.

'The widening gap between communication rich and poor, who seem unneeded as communicators or consumers, is the most obvious source of conflict. Abundance is, of course, relative; abundance for some is scarcity or nothing for others.'
Keane, John. (1998) 'The Humbling of the Intellectuals. Public Life in the Era of Communicative Abundance' in *Times Literary Supplement*. London, 28 August 1998.

18 The following descriptions of the legal situation in Zimbabwe builds, to a large degree, on Ndlela, Nkosinathi. (1997) 'Press Freedom and its Limits. The Law and the Media in Zimbabwe.' Unpublished M.Phil. Dissertation, Department of Media and Communication, University of Oslo; and Ndlela, Nkosinathi. (2001) 'Press Freedom and Democracy in Southern Africa. A comparative study of media laws in Zimbabwe and South Africa.' Ph.D. Thesis, University of Oslo; and Feltoe, Geoff. (1984) *A Guide to Press Law in Zimbabwe*. Harare: Legal Resources Foundation.

19 This account is based on reports in the electronic versions of *The Independent, The Standard, The Financial Gazette* and *Mail & Guardian*, as well as reports filed by the Harare IPS office.

20 Report on *Roundtable on Promoting Free, Independent and Pluralistic Media in Southern Africa and Discussions on the Establishment of a Regional Secretariat for The Media Institute of Southern Africa (MISA)*. Windhoek, 1992.

21 In an article in the Zimbabwean independent weekly the *Financial Gazette* (26 November 1992) on 'Zimbabwe's Constitution is Undemocratic and Unfair', Austin Chakaodza echoes this position in the following argument:
'While press freedom should exist within the confines of the socio-cultural make-up of society, editors must be allowed leeway in their presentation of news and ought to do so without fear for retribution by the powers that be. However, experience in Third World countries has shown that State control over the media extends not only towards control of media material but also over the editorial mind.'

22 Nordenstreng, Kaarle. (1995) 'Introduction: A State of the Art' in *European Journal of Communication (Special Issue on Media Ethics)*. Vol. 10, No. 4, December 1995.

23 Christians, Clifford G., Fackler, Mark and Rotzoll, Kim B. (1995) *Media Ethics: Cases and Moral Reasoning*. White Plains, NY: Longmans.

24 The following is based on points made in Wilson, John. (1996) *Understanding Journalism: A Guide to Issues*. London, New York: Routledge. (*See* Chapter 3.)

25 *Financial Gazette*, 23 July 1998.

26 For an analysis of this development, see Tomaselli, Keyan G. (1996) 'Globalisation and Localisation: The Political Economy of Shifting South African Media Identities.' Paper presented at the Conference on Identities, Democracy, Culture and Communication in Southern Africa. University of Natal, Durban, 4–9 February 1997.

27 The next two chapters are based on Nordenstreng, Kaarle. (1998) 'Professional Ethics: Between Fortress Journalism and Cosmopolitan Democracy' in Brants, Kees, Hermes, Joke and Van Zoonen, Liesbet (eds). (1998) *The Media in Question. Popular Cultures and Public Interests.* London, Thousand Oaks, New Dehli: Sage Publications; and Laitiila, Tiina. 'Journalistic Codes of Ethics in Europe' in *European Journal of Communication.* Vol. 10, No. 4, December 1995.

28 'State to Crack Whip on Independent Press' in *Parade.* November 1992.

29 'Parliament Witch-Hunt Challenged' in *Horizon.* December 1992.

30 *See* Gale, W.D. (undated) *The Rhodesian Press. The History of The Rhodesian Printing and Publishing Company Ltd.* Salisbury: Harare. (pp. 145–152)

31 Jonathan, Moyo. 'Time to Put Our House in Order' in *Horizon.* December 1992.

32 One example of such a critical and informed form of reporting is: Toolis, Kevin. (1998) 'Africa's Famine is very big business' in *Mail & Guardian.* 18–24 September 1998.

33 Belsey, Andrew and Chadwick, Ruth. 'Ethics and Politics in the Media: The Quest for Control' in Belsey, Andrew and Chadwick, Ruth (eds). (1992) *Ethical Issues in Journalism and the Media.* London, New York: Routledge. (pp. 4–5, 14)

Media Ethics
Teacher's Guide

Nordic SADC Journalism Centre

Francis P. Kasoma
Professor of Journalism and Mass Communication
University of Zambia

INTRODUCTION

Teaching journalism ethics to journalists who are already working is a very demanding task. First, they have already formed certain habits in their journalistic practice, some of which work against their ethical formation. Second, their theoretical knowledge of what constitutes ethical matters may have been influenced by either the training they had (if they are trained journalists) or the outlook on ethics by their media houses and/or their peers.

The training of journalists in SADC countries has very rarely treated journalism ethics as a separate subject or course. What is often offered at colleges, polytechnics and universities that have journalism programmes, are essentially courses in journalism law with a sprinkling of some ethical aspects. The courses are variously called 'Journalism Law and Ethics', 'Media Law and Ethics', or simply 'Journalism/Media Law'.

The course participants are likely to have gone through training that has left them with the idea that journalism ethics is an appendage of journalism law, and that if one understands journalism law, one automatically knows all about journalism ethics. The aim of this course is to bring journalism ethics into focus as a very important issue in journalism, distinct from journalism law.

The writers of this manual had two options, which teachers should know about in order to use the course modules effectively. One option was to work out a complete and independent course, like any of the other nine courses offered by the Nordic SADC Journalism Centre:

- Foreign reporting;
- Political reporting;
- Reporting the community and local government;
- Rural reporting;
- Reporting the national economy;
- Business reporting;
- Media management;
- Gender; and
- Computer systems.

The other option was to work out a course that was partly independent in terms of its theoretical base, and supportive or complementary of the other courses, offering the ethical applications of whatever course was being conducted. For example, participants of the foreign reporting course would be taught general ethical theories and the application of these theories to foreign reporting. For practical purposes, the second option was chosen.

The modules of this course are therefore taught as part of whatever course is being taught. The expectation is that the teachers who are teaching the other courses should also be able to teach the ethics components of those courses (i.e. the practical applications of the ethical theories to the particular courses being taught).

It is advisable, however, that should a teacher feel that he or she cannot handle the ethics component, someone conversant with the subject is hired to teach it.

THEORETICAL BACKGROUND

In teaching the theoretical background to journalism ethics, it is important that the teacher gives a broad view of the key issues, which include the following:

- The definition and discussion of the concept of press freedom, without which a treatise on journalism ethics would be meaningless. Questioning ethical performance only makes sense if the journalist is free to choose various journalistic behaviours. The discussion would have to include special considerations on censorship (both imposed and self-), which should not be mixed up with the concept of professional judgement by journalists to publish or not to publish certain information. It would also have to include the debate concerning press freedom and new media technologies. Finally, the teacher should include in this section a discussion about how press freedom can be maintained and even improved. He or she should stress that freedom of the press, like democracy, is an ideal that can never be attained in its perfect form, but decreases or improves depending on how much pressure journalists exert on authorities, particularly governments, that have the power to restrict it. When journalists relax in their fight for press freedom, they will have less of it. Freedom of the press should also include giving the people (the citizens) free access to the media in order for them to express their opinions. It should include making the media accessible to the people when they want it. The current situation in most of Africa, where people living in towns have greater access to media than those living in rural areas, is a negation of press freedom.

- The definition of press freedom ought to be done with the requirements of democracy and democratic governance in mind; so the teacher ought to bring into the discussion the meaning of democracy and the role a free press plays in a democratic polity.

The teacher should stress that without a free press there can be no democracy because a free press is one of the four pillars of democracy, the other ones being Parliament or the Legislature, the Judiciary, and the Executive arm of government. These make democracy possible through a system of checks and balances.

One of the thorniest issues in African journalism, in the wake of multi-party politics, is defending the notion that democracy entails that the citizen, any citizen, has a right to start a newspaper or broadcasting station. In other words, the principle of freedom to disseminate ideas gives anybody a democratic right to practise some form of journalism. In the new democracies, there is a proliferation of private newspapers, most of which are edited and worked on by 'journalists' who are not trained but are merely exercising their democratic right of self-expression.

Teachers are likely to face an outcry from course participants that these 'gate-crashing' journalists should not be allowed to practise journalism, because they are messing it up by practising it unethically. This idea raises the issue of licensing journalists, which is clearly undemocratic.

However, if the pseudo-journalists are allowed to practise, the incidence of unethical journalism increases. This dilemma has led some African governments to try to enforce ethical journalism, by promulgating media council statutes introducing the licensing of journalists (thereby keeping untrained journalists out of the profession). Teachers should understand the dilemma if they are going to explain its intricacies to course participants.

- A discussion about the role of the press in (democratic) society should logically follow. Teachers should focus on the duties and responsibilities of a free press in a democratic society. They should stress that rights, which freedom always entails, should always be accompanied by duties and responsibilities that are, in turn, guided by values and principles. A free press owes it to society to perform certain functions to vindicate its freedom. An irresponsible press cannot enjoy its freedom for long. In other words, there is a causal link between freedom and responsibility. The discussion on the democratic functions of the press (the term is used generically to include both broadcast and print media) belongs here. Teachers need to link the necessity of citizens having access to information and how this enhances democracy. Democracy involves making choices between alternatives. However, a person who has little or no information available to him or her has very little chance of making meaningful choices and, as such, is deprived of fully participating in the democratic governance of his or her country.

At this point, teachers should discuss the broad functions of the press in society, as presented in the theoretical outline, and even move beyond the six functions given. One main function of the media that is not mentioned in the theoretical discussion, but is pertinent to the press in the developing world, particularly Africa, is that of the media preserving and promoting the culture of the society it serves. Be careful not to mislead course participants in explaining how the press should promote and preserve culture. To begin with, culture should be defined as a way of life of a given people. As such, it bears positive, negative and neutral aspects. The negative cultural aspects are those taboos, customs, practices, etc. that have outlived their usefulness. A good example is the requirement in some African societies that women should not eat eggs. The press has no business promoting and preserving such cultural practices. However, it does have a duty to promote and preserve positive and neutral cultural practices so that society can forge forward.

Another function not mentioned in the theoretical text section is that of advertising. Media advertising has become more complicated than merely the promotion of the sale of goods and services, which it used to be. It has become broader and may be described as the promotion of specific messages from individuals or organisations. The widespread use of funeral advertisements in the African press in the 1990s is a case in point. Funeral advertisements have nothing to do with the promotion of goods and services. They are sentimental expressions of attachment to those who have departed by living relatives and friends.

The point being made here is that teachers should not regard the itemised functions of the press in a democracy as exhaustive. There may be equally important functions that have not been discussed, which teachers may deem important to bring to the attention of course participants, particularly in political reporting, reporting on the community and local government, and rural reporting.

JOURNALISM ETHICS DEFINED

The next part of the background discussion should involve defining the meaning of journalism ethics. This could be discussed within the socio-cultural context of society, starting with Euro-American culture and moving on to African society. This discussion would have to include a general discussion about what journalism ethics is and why it is important. The notions of ethical principles and values would have to be introduced. So should the debate about the ethical yardsticks that journalists use to measure the 'ethicalness' of their actions. A growing body of literature on the African outlook on ethics is available, to which teachers can refer (*see* Bibliography).

The next logical step in the discussion should be about the universally accepted elements of concern in journalism ethics. These should be drawn from both the Euro-American and the African approaches to journalism ethics discussed above. Universally accepted elements of journalism ethics can also be deduced from both local and international codes of ethics of media houses and journalists' associations.

In the African context, it is important to discuss whether laws can enforce media ethics or not. This is important in view of the ongoing attempts by many African countries, particularly those in the SADC region, to promulgate laws on media or press councils, which, it is hoped, should enable journalists to behave more responsibly. Teachers should stress that journalism ethics is first and foremost a personal commitment to doing what is morally acceptable as one performs journalistic tasks. Personal journalistic ethical considerations begin where elements within a moral system conflict and a person is called upon to choose between the alternatives. A journalist may find himself or herself trying to reconcile the various conflicting ethical tenets to which he or she personally ascribes (e.g. religious, social, cultural and political ethical commitments). There are also organisational ethical pressures on the journalist arising from his or her allegiance to a media house employer. A media house would usually demand of its journalists certain ethical standards. Finally, the journalism profession usually requires that journalists belonging to journalists' associations should adhere to some specific ethical codes imposed on them by these bodies. In teaching this section, teachers should point out that journalism is more of a group than an individual profession, and that ethical dictates of the media house or journalists' association nearly always supersede those of the individual journalist whenever the two are in conflict. The presence of regional and even world journalists' associations further strengthens journalists' approach to enforcing ethics as a professional group. These regional and world journalists' bodies lend credence to the existence of global ethical values and principles.

NORMATIVE THEORIES OF THE PRESS AND JOURNALISM ETHICS

Teachers should undertake linking the normative theories of the press to the discussion of journalism ethics. They should not regard the four theories propounded by Siebert, Peterson and Schramme in their book *Four Theories of the Press*, published more than forty years ago, as the only theories that can be used to anchor a treatise of journalism ethics. Attention should be paid to theories that were developed later, such as development journalism theory, direct and indirect media control theory (developed by Asante, et al.), and neo-multiparty theory (Kasoma,1999). Kasoma's theory, in particular, explains a lot about what is happening in the press in Africa.

Teachers should not give the impression that normative theories of the press, such as Soviet communist theory, end with the fall of the regimes that gave rise to them. The authoritarian theory of the press, for example, continued long after Europe's dictators were gone. Similarly, the Soviet communist theory has remnants, not only in the states of the former Soviet Union, but also in those states in developing countries, particularly in Africa, that emulated the Soviet press system. Press theories have a tendency to overlap. As new theories come to the fore, the ones that formed the status quo are still present in some form. The best example teachers could use is that of Africa's emerging democracies, which have yet to shed their dictatorial and authoritarian tendencies in their relations with the press, both private and government-owned. The ethical implications for a country or press system adopting a particular normative theoretical approach should be discussed briefly. More attention should be focused on the normative theories that are dominant in Africa today. However, do not underplay theories that may not be dominant now, but have the potential of being so, or were dominant in the past.

GOVERNMENT AND PRIVATE PRESS

A course in journalism ethics with particular reference to SADC countries, or to the whole of Africa for that matter, should discuss the ethical implications of having a dual press system: private and government press. Teachers should be careful not to create the impression that all is well with the private press in performing their democratic roles of ensuring good governance by making those in power accountable and transparent for their actions or the lack of them. The misuse of press freedom by the private press should also be discussed, including sensationalism, 'vendetta journalism', etc.

Ethical problems faced by the government press should also be discussed, particularly censorship. The effects of censorship on the professional performance of journalists working for the government press should be seen in the broad ethical perspective of short-changing the people who, through taxes, are made to support these media, which ultimately only serve the purpose of the ruling class. It should also be seen as destroying the morale of many young journalists who, for fear of being punished, give up the idea of investigative journalism and settle for the easier and less dangerous 'speech-reporting' of ministers and other government officials.

Teachers should broaden the discussion to consider the effects of press ownership on media ethics. Take care not to let the discussion degenerate into accusing the private press or any other form of press ownership, save that of government, of censorship. Because of the need for the press to make governments accountable and transparent, censorship of the press by those in government poses much more danger to democratic governance than that practised by private – and other – forms of press. In other words, the ethical consequences of government censorship of the press are more devastating to democracy than the ramifications of the private press deciding which information to publish and which not to publish.

The ethical issue of censorship should be discussed in full. Teachers should explain that there are three types of censorship:

- *Pre-publication censorship*, sometimes known as 'prior restraint', prevents the publication or broadcasting of certain information. Pre-publication censorship can also take the form of forcing journalists to publish information which compromises their professional integrity. The pressure used, particularly by government, takes many forms, ranging from threats to make reporters and the media houses 'pay' for recalcitrant behaviour, through some form of punishment, to promises of rewards for being 'obedient'. Essentially, the 'carrot and stick' method is used to enforce pre-publication censorship.
- *Post-publication censorship* occurs when those in authority, particularly government, punish journalists and media houses for publishing or broadcasting or not publishing or broadcasting information demanded by them. Punishment may range from losing one's job, to being incarcerated or even killed.
- *Self-censorship* takes place when the selection of what to and what not to publish/broadcast is influenced by fear of punishment, even

though there is no overt pressure by the authorities on the journalists. Teachers should clearly explain the difference between professional judgement and self-censorship. When journalists decide, not out of fear, but out of journalistic professional considerations, whether or not to publish or broadcast a story, they are exercising their right of professional judgement and not practising self-censorship.

ETHICAL FRAMEWORK OF MEDIA LAW

The enforcement of journalism ethics by law should be considered an exception rather than the rule. The State has no business legislating for the enforcement of journalism ethics. The enforcement of journalism ethics should, therefore, be left to the journalists. However, the State, as custodian of people's rights, has a duty to protect rights that are persistently flouted by a section of society, journalists included. In other words, while allowing journalists as professionals to enforce their own ethics, the State still has a responsibility, when it sees that journalists are impinging on other rights in their expression of press freedom, to legislate to protect those rights that are being endangered. However, this should only be done after the State has called on journalists to respect the rights of other people and the journalists refuse to do so. Even then, journalists can still protest and refuse to obey the law if they conscientiously feel that it encroaches on their right to practise ethical journalism. Such a deadlock could be settled by having recourse to courts of law.

The title of this section, 'Ethical framework of media law', presupposes the fact that any law the government passes should facilitate the ethical performance of journalists, rather than merely calling on them to obey the law for law's sake. An ethical journalist would not flout the human rights of others, unless it was absolutely necessary and an exceptional situation. A good example of this is the revelation of information by a journalist that deprives a few people of certain basic human rights while protecting and enhancing the same rights for the majority of the people. Using legal logic, it would still be illegal for a journalist to deprive the few people of their basic human rights. Teachers should stress that *what is legal may not necessarily be ethical, what is ethical can sometimes be illegal, and what is legal can also be ethical.*

This is an appropriate point for teachers to discuss the numerous attempts by governments within the SADC region to pass media council statutes, which, as items of legislation, conflict with the general observance of journalism ethics, hence the outcry by journalists in almost every country not to have them passed as law.

Teachers will also find it useful to discuss the very serious problem, found in almost every SADC country, of supposedly democratic governments clinging on to outdated laws affecting journalists that were promulgated either by the very dictatorial governments they condemned and replaced, or by the equally undemocratic colonial regimes. Teachers should point out that these outdated laws are hindering rather than enhancing the practice of ethical journalism and should be repealed or substantially amended to reflect democratic governance.

The law on defamation is a good example with regard to former British colonies in the SADC region. Nearly all the legislation on defamation in these countries is based on the UK's Defamation Act of 1953. The UK has substantially amended this Act, whereas its former colonies have kept the same wording and, hence, the same spirit of the law that is meant to severely punish the journalist (even when civil libel is in question) for causing someone to be hated, held in contempt, despised or lowered in his or her profession, or lose business due to the libellous publication of information. The emphasis is on teaching the journalist and the media a lesson if he or she is found to have broken the defamation law either as a tort or as a crime. In some SADC countries, there is even legislation against defaming the Head of State (again bequeathed from the UK), which, because it is subject to interpretation by government, the supposed victim, tends to be too widely interpreted, encroaching on peoples' right to know.

Moreover, out of all the SADC countries, only in South Africa and Namibia, is press freedom enshrined in the constitution as a basic and inalienable human right, not just affecting journalists, but also the general populace. Most of the constitutions merely protect freedom of expression as a human right, which they erroneously equate or claim includes the right to a free press.

Teachers should indicate to course participants the distinction between the right to a free press and the right to free expression. Point out that, where the right to a free press has been enshrined in the constitution as a basic human right, journalists and members of the public can challenge the government and parliament in courts of law if they do anything to contravene it. In other words, they have the legal backing of the supreme law of the land to challenge government actions that contravene press freedom. Some countries, such as Zambia, have included in their constitutions, more or less as an afterthought, a statement on press freedom which, when read in context, is meaningless. This is because it is mentioned in connection with freedom of expression, when the two should be clearly distinguished.

Moreover, in the Zambian case, the inconsistency becomes apparent when more than ten situations are listed in the section stating when freedom of expression should be curtailed. Those who amended the constitution (it has been amended four times since independence in 1964) gave freedom of expression with one hand and then withdrew it with the other, saying practically nothing about freedom of the press. There was no need to list these exceptions, particularly when they are subject to interpretation by the same government that wants to see freedom of expression diminished.

All of these aspects can be discussed in terms of the ethical framework of media law. Kasoma discusses in full the implications of trying to enforce media ethics by law in *Equid Novi* (1996).

FREEDOM OF INFORMATION LAWS

The need for freedom of information laws becomes apparent where governments persistently deny citizens information they are supposed to have in the spirit of democratic transparency and accountability. Generally, governments are not known for their generosity in supplying information to the press. However, when the press seeks particular information, governments are bound by the democratic requirement of good governance to give it, unless they have very good reasons – for example, in the interest of public security – to withhold it. A freedom of information law places the onus of proving that withholding the information is in the public interest in the hands of the government. All journalists need to do is to state to the court that they are seeking specific information that the public has a right to know, and that the government is refusing to release it.

Teachers should not flinch from pointing out that nearly all the governments in the SADC region refuse to cooperate with journalists seeking state information. Only a freedom of information law would rectify the situation. However, the law needs to be enforced by strong, independent courts, which are able to stand firm and demand that the government releases the information, if it (the government) fails to prove that it is in the interests of the public not to release it. Not all of the SADC states have such strong and independent courts.

The biggest hindrance to the people's right to know in most of the SADC countries is the presence of the Official Secrets law, which is a relic of the colonial governments. Because the interpretation of what constitutes a secret is left to the governments of the day, journalists often find information about government dealings labelled 'Official

Secret'. Nearly every government file is marked 'Secret' or 'Top Secret', and reporters who seek information from these files risk being prosecuted for contravening the Official Secrets Act, as do government officials who leak information. African journalists from former British colonies are, therefore, constantly in danger of contravening this notorious Act and being prosecuted. They work in fear, not knowing when they may be accused of contravening the Act.

Teachers should point out the usefulness of the D-Notices in the UK, which warn British journalists that they may be prosecuted for contravening the Official Secrets Act if they publish specific information. Although British media houses often ignore the D-Notices, they are at least forewarned of the possibility of breaking this notorious law and can adequately prepare for their defence should they decide to ignore them. Journalists within the former British colonies need to rally the people to fight for the abrogation of, or at least the substantive amendment of the Official Secrets Act as it is an enemy of the people's right to know. It is clear that the Official Secrets Act and the Freedom of Information Act cannot exist side by side.

Discussing the two Acts should lead into the subject of the ethical requirement of journalists to protect their sources. When journalists are compelled by the courts to name their sources – for example, during an Official Secrets trial – they should not name the sources if they promised not to reveal them, even if the courts threaten to send them to jail for refusing.

Teachers need to carefully explain the ethical requirement of journalists not to name their sources, if this is what has been agreed. However, generally in journalistic reporting, reporters have an obligation to the people to name their sources. This is not what we see in SADC journalism today. Newspapers in particular are full of stories in which anonymous sources are quoted. This type of journalism risks destroying a person's life (defamation) by publishing allegations from an anonymous source. Moreover, the accused person is rarely given a chance to defend him- or herself against unknown accusers. Even worse, journalists are encouraging dishonest people to make serious allegations against other people and then hide behind anonymity. This is frequently the case in political mudslinging, which has become common in SADC countries, particularly during election time.

Journalists are only ethically bound not to name their sources in the few, exceptional cases when they and their source agree that the source will suffer some serious inconvenience, such as being fired, suspended or prosecuted for giving the information. Unfortunately, the exception seems to have become the rule in the SADC journalism of the 1990s and into the twenty-first century. The trend should be reversed, and those taking journalism ethics courses such as this one should be at the forefront of helping to return the situation to normality. At this point, teachers should discuss other laws that infringe on freedom of the press. Since the class will be composed of participants from various SADC countries, it is better to discuss laws that are common to as many of the countries as possible.

Defamation

Teachers should be wary of discussing journalism ethical requirements that are also embedded in law. The aim should be to discuss the ethical requirements rather than the requirements of law, which should be covered adequately in a media law course.

In terms of the ethical requirements of a journalist not to defame people, discussion should begin with a general understanding of what defamation is and why it is ethically unacceptable. Defamation should be defined and the various parts of the definition explained carefully to the course participants. Teachers should include in the definition the components that are common to all SADC countries, and not try to look at the way each country has tried to define defamation. The differences between defamation, libel and slander should be carefully explained.

Defamation is a general term that encompasses libel and slander. *Libel* is defamation in a permanent form, including publication or broadcasting. *Slander* is defamation in a temporary form, usually the spoken word. Broadcasting qualifies as libel and not slander because, although it deals in the spoken word, generally there are written scripts that broadcasters read or follow. There is also the master tape, which broadcasting stations are required to keep by law, which records and retains everything that was broadcast for the day. These two points preserve what is broadcast in a permanent form. Moreover, the broadcast media (radio and television) have, given their wide circulation, been seen to inflict the defamation sting more than, for example, newspapers, and this is treated as libel, which is a more serious form of defamation than slander.

Defamation relating to computer communication mediums (i.e. the Internet) would also qualify as libel. In future, libel suits arising from computer-based publications are likely to increase substantively as the computer takes centre stage in mass communication.

Teachers should then discuss the very important ethical question arising from the conflict between the need not to libel a person and the equally important right of the public to know, right to property, right to life, etc. In other words, the media face the choice not to libel someone and deny people the information they have a right to, or making libellous information available to people because they have a right to know it.

A good example that can be used to illustrate this dilemma is the choice to reveal the identity of a person with HIV/AIDS, who has gone on a spree infecting others, and the need to preserve his or her right to privacy, by not revealing his or her identity.

Teachers should be careful not to give straightforward, clear-cut answers to ethical problems. The circumstances of each case should be examined and a logical conclusion reached that the journalist can defend. Teachers should stress to the course participants that ethical problems are rarely set out in black and white. There are often grey areas, which make the issue more complicated than it appears. Many libel situations have twists and turns that require cautious and informed judgement to reach an ethically sound decision.

It is important to let the class discuss issues before arriving at conclusions. Good ethical reasoning requires the facts of the circumstances to be established. The values and ethical principles at stake, both for and against, should then be examined. The journalist should finally decide which of these values and principles to give his or her allegiance to. This will determine the ethical situation logically. Ethical judgements based on emotions rather than reason often prove unsound.

Teachers can give the course participant examples of how they could find themselves libelling someone through journalistic reportage. There are ethical (and in this case, legal) requirements in order for libel to take place:

- The publication of material that is clearly libellous. If the material published is not clearly libellous, according to the definition of libel, there can be no genuine complaint for libel.
- The plaintiff should be clearly identified in the libellous material that has been published. Here, the discussion should focus on the various formulae journalists use to mask the identity of someone who is the subject of libellous material. The formulae include: not naming the source, and using descriptions that do not make his or her identity obvious – for example, 'a highly placed government official'. However, course participants should be warned that some of the formulae meant to mask the identity of a source could actually reveal that person's identity – for example, when a reporter refers to the 'highest government official' in a certain province or town. Often there is only one such official in a small town and everybody knows who it is.

The two main types of libel should also be taught: libel *per se* and libel *per quod* (sometimes known as 'unintentional libel'). Libel *per se* applies when the meaning of the offending words or material (e.g. a painting) are libellous in themselves, without explanation. Libel *per quod* is when the words or material become libellous because of extrinsic factors and circumstances known to the plaintiff, the defendant, and the reasonable or ordinary person in the street. For example, calling a woman a 'Monica Lewinsky' may be libellous where such association is regarded by people in the community as suggesting promiscuity with people who hold high office.

Teachers should then explain the various ways in which libel can be mitigated. In other words, once the reporter has libelled someone, how can the sting be reduced? Aspects such as apologies, retractions, clarifications, etc. should be discussed, emphasising the fact that the harm done to the plaintiff cannot really be removed completely.

Teachers should point out to the course participants that, depending on the way they are worded and published or broadcast, apologies, retractions and clarifications may actually repeat the libel and, therefore, cause more harm than good.

Two types of apologies, retractions and clarifications can be identified. First, there is the type where the media house and the journalist realise they have libelled someone and, before the person complains, apologises, retracts or clarifies what has been published. In this way, the journalist and the media house show that they are sorry for what they did and that they intended no malice. This is usually the case with unintentional libel. By the time the mass-medium house receives a complaint, if it receives one at all, the plaintiff would have been pacified to some extent.

The second type of apology, retraction or clarification is done after the plaintiff has complained. This usually requires that the wording and the manner of publication or broadcasting is agreed upon by both parties. If litigation is foreseen, such agreement may involve lawyers representing both parties.

Teachers should emphasise that what matters is the good will and understanding shown by the journalist towards the injured party. The attitude that journalists are infallible and do not make mistakes does not augur well with the ethical way of dealing with libel.

Consider the traditional defences of libel, not with the aim of getting journalists out of trouble (which would be the legal approach), but rather by ensuring that the fear for libel does not stand in the way of journalists publishing information that people have the right to know. If the journalists know how they can argue a case successfully, to show that they have not libelled the person who has complained, they will not be afraid of exposing seemingly libellous information to people when they have a right to know about it.

The three traditional defences for libel are: justification, fair comment and qualified privilege, each of which has ethical implications.

Justification means proving that what has been alleged is true and factual. Truth reporting or 'sticking to the facts' is an ethical requirement of all journalists. Reporting based on falsehoods or lies is unethical. Justification is a defence that is based on the assumption that, if the allegation is true, the harm done to the plaintiff is minimal. The understanding is that that person's honour and respect has already been compromised by the behaviour being reported. The honour or integrity that libel suits want to protect is not the self-image of the person being libelled, but rather his or her public image. If other people know for a fact that what is being reported about that person is true, the honour and integrity of that person is already compromised by his or her behaviour and not by the press.

However, the truth required for the defence of justification is substantive truth, which is not easy to obtain. For example, if the allegation is that someone stole public funds, it is not enough to show that the allegation was made by so-and-so, who confirms that the allegation as published by the press came from him or her, meaning that the press reported accurately. What must be proved is that the person in fact stole the money by, for example, showing that person a cheque that was cashed in his or her name.

The defence of *fair comment* is based on the need for the press to comment on matters of public interest, so that the public can debate them (set the agenda) to find solutions. The defence of fair comment should be based on truth (fact) and fairness in a matter of public interest. But the truth or fact required here is less rigid than that required for justification. It is enough to show that the allegation was made by someone who confirms that he or she made it. However, the matter being commented upon should be in the public interest. Finally, the comment should be fair and not biased or favouring one side.

The defence of *qualified privilege* applies when journalists report fairly and accurately what is said by government executives ex-officio. Such government executives enjoy absolute privilege for saying what they say, while journalists enjoy qualified privilege. If journalists do not report such officers fairly and accurately, qualified privilege does not apply. For example, if the Head of State publicly and officially calls someone a thief and the journalist reports this accurately, while simultaneously giving the accused party the opportunity to say something in his or her defence (fairness), such a report is not libellous and, therefore, not actionable.

Teaching libel as an ethical issue involves encouraging journalists to realise that they should be considerate, and not unnecessarily destroy other people's reputations as they carry out their tasks. Journalism is a profession that provides a service to society and is not one in which some people are persecuted just for the sake of it.

Pressure from government

The question of whether government can force journalists to be ethical by applying pressure on them is a pertinent one, especially for SADC countries where this seems to be common. Outside the law, governments have no business whatsoever trying to enforce journalism ethics, unless they themselves are media operators. Theoretically, therefore, governments can enforce journalism ethics for the media they own and operate (i.e. government media). They cannot do the same for the private media, where ethical responsibility lies in the hands (partly) of the people operating these media.

But even for the government-owned and -controlled media, which are anachronisms and should not be allowed in an African democratic society, the idea that the person in the dock should be the one controlling the behaviour of the judge is ethically unacceptable unless certain mechanisms are in place. The press, regardless of who owns it, should be an instrument of democracy, providing the necessary checks and balances to specifically make government transparent and accountable to the people. This is not possible when the same government determines how journalists and media houses should ethically perform their functions.

It is, therefore, important for teachers to teach the four ways in which journalism ethics, outside the law, should be enforced.

First, a journalist should have a sense of responsibility and a conscience not to hurt others unnecessarily while performing his or her journalistic duties. As pointed out earlier, a journalist's ethical standing takes into consideration his or her personal allegiances (e.g. religious affiliation, personal character, etc.).

Secondly, the mass-medium house has a right to demand certain ethical behaviour from its journalists.

Thirdly, a professional journalists' association or union has a right to demand that its members comply with certain ethical requirements. Journalists' associations usually have ethical codes of conduct.

Fourthly, members of the public have a right to demand ethical behaviour from journalists. The media houses and journalists work to produce a product for the public and, if they are not happy with the way this is done or with the product itself, they should say so and demand better performance and better products.

Demanding better ethical performance is one thing; enforcing it is quite another. Members of the public can also enforce ethical performance. For example, they can make it clear to the journalists and the media houses that they do not like the way they are behaving and that, if they do not stop, they would apply sanctions. Sanctions may include a mass boycott of the offending media products (e.g. refusing to buy the newspaper or listening to the radio station until the journalists, media houses and the public reach some agreement about proper behaviour). Such pressure or mass action from society is, however, not feasible in the SADC regions, where most members of the public are not particularly 'media literate' (meaning that they are not knowledgeable about their rights with regard to the media and reporters). Teachers should point out that, for people in the SADC countries to become 'media literate', there should be some form of 'education' carried out mainly through the media. The argument that government officers are also members of the public and, therefore, entitled to demand and enforce ethical performance of journalists is not valid because of the reason stated earlier: that the government is in the dock and the accused cannot pass judgement on the judge (the media and journalists).

JOURNALISM ETHICS WITHIN THE INSTITUTIONAL FRAMEWORK

It is important for teachers to emphasise that journalism is more of a team or group profession than an individual profession. Journalists are, therefore, bound by the ethical requirements of the media houses they work for or the journalists' professional group or association they belong to.

However, media houses also have ethical responsibilities towards journalists, including giving them unqualified protection in the performance of their duties. An editor who betrays his or her reporters acts unethically. Similarly, an editor who practices self-censorship not only deprives the public of information they have a right to know, but also instils in reporters a fear or despair of not carrying out investigative journalism.

Teachers should point out that the media houses have a duty to facilitate the ethical performance of journalists working for them. Managers should insist on getting the best from their journalists. If a reporter, for example, habitually files half-completed stories that are inaccurate and untruthful, the editor should insist that that person improves his or her performance. While this would certainly make life difficult for the lazy reporter, it would end up improving the ethical performance for not only the journalist but also the other reporters who witness the pressures to which their unethical colleague is being subjected.

Editorial responsibility requires that the editor shoulder the blame for the bad (unethical) performance of his or her journalists publicly, while privately (within the media house) ensuring that reporters become more responsible in their reportage. Editorial responsibility also requires that the editor does not let his or her mass-media house become prone to unethical practices, such as reporters accepting bribes.

Other forms of editorial responsibility should also be brought to the attention of course participants – for example, providing transport to reporters to carry out their assignments. The practice in many SADC countries of reporters, particularly those working for government media, accompanying government ministers and other officers to rural areas exposes reporters to the unethical practice of biased reporting.

MEDIA AND COMMERCIALISM

Teachers should link the discussion on media and commercialism to that of freedom of the press. The media need to be commercially viable to survive on the competitive market as independent institutions. However, where the media have to rely on government grants and/or subsidies, its freedom is often compromised. To complicate the issue, commercially viable media are not necessarily free to make editorial and other journalistic decisions. Owners often meddle in the policies of the particular media in order to gain political and commercial advantage in the areas in which their businesses have been established.

Teachers need to explain these paradoxes with particular reference to the media in southern Africa. Examples from outside the SADC region should also be used to clarify the issues, particularly where local ones cannot be obtained. These will be useful when this module is taught within the context of the course on international reporting.

In many SADC states, where governments are unable to find adequate funds to support the government-owned and -controlled mass media, these media should supplement their income for survival by becoming partly commercial. Some media watchers in southern Africa have seen this as an attempt by the government to eradicate the private media. Consequently, the democratic principle of availing the people with pluralist media to enable them to have access to divergent views and information may not be realised. Teachers should conclude from this discussion that it is unethical for journalists, particularly editors, working for government media to compete unfairly with the private media by becoming partly commercial while still benefiting from government subsidies.

Those belonging to the government media camp who are aware that some Nordic countries also have a system where government gives grants to private media, argue that they do not see anything wrong with government media in Africa also receiving 'commercial support' while enjoying government subsidies. Teachers should refute such arguments by pointing out that the government grants in Nordic countries are applied in a system with established democratic traditions. The basic philosophy is that government has a duty to facilitate the provision of essential services to its people and that the provision of information by the media is considered one such essential service. The government has to step in and assist if a particular mass medium is facing some problems in providing this service.

The media that receive government grants are carefully selected and must meet certain criteria, including wide circulation. Such media retain their editorial independence and often put the same government that gave them the grant under the microscope to fulfil their democratic duty of making government accountable and transparent to the people. The situation is different, however, with African governments that fail to support the media they own and ask them to cut into the commercial cake, thereby depriving the private media industry of its source of livelihood.

Teachers should explain clearly the concepts of a public broadcaster and publicly owned media, with reference to southern Africa. Where publicly owned media operate successfully, mechanisms are always in place to ensure that these media are not answerable to the government of the day. These include the use of radio and television licences as a source of support for publicly owned broadcast stations. Where the State gives grants to such media, the funds are administered by the National Assembly (Parliament) through one of its committees, and are not provided by a government ministry – for example, information and broadcasting – as part of its budget. This is because, where the subvention for a mass medium house comes from a government ministry, there is always the tendency for allegiance to the government of the day.

This is the case with most of the so-called broadcasting corporations in SADC countries. They are corporations by name, but heavily dependent on the government for their editorial decisions and day-to-day operations.

Advertising and marketing

Although advertising is not strictly part of journalism, its operations affect journalism, making it a valid ethical issue. In teaching the ethical effects of advertising on journalism, therefore, teachers should approach the issue thematically, after giving a general introduction about the role of advertising and its place in journalism. The following themes should be discussed:

- The need to separate editorial material and advertisements is both important and necessary in southern Africa, where many people cannot tell the difference between an advertisement and a news story or feature. For them, what a newspaper publishes or a radio station broadcasts is treated, without any discrimination, as news and information from the newspaper or the radio. The idea that people outside the newspaper or radio station can have their information published or broadcast as advertisements, over which journalists have no control, is not easily understood.

- The ratio of advertising to news should not favour advertising, thereby depriving people of a variety of news and other information. This becomes a serious ethical issue, particularly where the price of a newspaper is very high, as is the case in most southern African countries. The issue becomes one of whether people are paying for the advertisements or the news and other information (features) that the newspaper contains, which has been reduced to the minimum.

- What constitutes a free advertisement or plug and an editorial write-up is often not clearly differentiated. The two should be clearly differentiated to prevent media consumers from being misled.

- Advertisers should not try to influence journalists, particularly editors, in making editorial decisions that favour them and adversely affect editorial content. This is particularly the case when advertisers put pressure on journalists (editors) to publish or not publish certain information because it is favourable or unfavourable to their advertising interests and/or market.

- There is the temptation to increase circulation or listernership/viewership through sensationalism to attract more advertising and, therefore, greater advertising revenue. This is brought about by the principle that the bigger the circulation or listernership/viewership, the more advertisers will be attracted to advertise, and higher advertising rates can be charged. Sensationalism is unethical because it falsifies the truth.

- Political advertising disguised as editorial material can have adverse effects on the democratic process in southern Africa. However, even in cases where they are identified, the messages they contain may be highly deceptive since they are not subject to journalistic editing. Thousands of people can end up being misled.

- Disguising advertisements as editorial material has become a very serious issue, particularly in newspaper supplements and shopping guides on radio and television.

CODES OF ETHICAL CONDUCT IN JOURNALISM

A good starting point in teaching codes of ethical conduct in journalism is a debate on rights and responsibilities. Rights must be accompanied by duties and responsibilities. In journalism, the right to a free press only makes sense if corresponding duties and responsibilities are imposed on journalists. Part of these duties and responsibilities are expressed in codes of ethical conduct.

It is important, however, for teachers to point out that codes of ethical conduct in journalism do not cover all possible ethical permutations and situations. How could they? They are merely an expression of some of the duties and responsibilities of journalists to society. Teachers should discuss the debates about the usefulness of codes of ethical conduct in journalism. These include:

- those who argue that there should be no codes because they do not change anything, and because journalists continually flout them;
- those who argue (particularly tabloid journalists) that codes of conduct cannot be generalised; each media house will decide what is best for it and its journalists; and
- those who argue that codes of conduct are ideals that cannot be attained, but are useful models that journalists should aim for if they are to be ethical journalists.

Journalism ethics involves more than what is contained in the codes of conduct. It is a commitment to doing the morally right thing in all possible circumstances and permutations.

However, as a means of self-regulation by journalists, codes of conduct are very useful because they stem attempts by governments to enforce journalism ethics by passing laws. Government interventions always restrict press freedom instead of enhancing it. This is because, in nearly all African countries, particularly those in the SADC region, the most common laws concerning journalists and the mass media that are promulgated are restrictive. Rarely are enabling laws passed that positively give journalists rights, privileges and responsibilities.

One of the best approaches to teaching codes of ethical conduct is to make the various codes available to the course participants and ask them to identify common denominators. Debate whether these common denominators constitute what could be called universal ethical values for journalists.

It should also be pointed out that the ultimate beneficiaries of codes of conduct are the public and not journalists; adhering to the codes is an attempt by the journalists to serve the public better. This is why it is useful, when defining a mechanism to enforce these codes, that members of the public are included.

Teachers should present to course participants mechanisms for the voluntary enforcement of codes of conduct by journalists. These include voluntary press councils, journalists' associations or unions at local and international levels, and at media house level.

SOME ETHICAL ISSUES DISCUSSED

In this section, teachers should be flexible and not be tied only to the issues covered in the book. Other issues are equally central.

- *Public interest v The right to privacy* Teachers should explain what public interest and the right to privacy mean, and their relationship in a democratic polity. Be careful not to make one of these rights sound more important than the other, as this would bias the course participants into thinking that the 'more important one' should always be promoted at the expense of the other.
- *Decency and good taste* This is another controversial topic that should be presented carefully and always discussed within the cultural context – in this case, African culture.
- *Conflict of interest* The honest way for journalists is to not report on anything in which they have a conflict of interest. This includes an emotional relationship between the journalist and the source, be it positive or negative.
- *Subterfuge* Journalists posing as other functionaries (e.g. police officers or intelligence officials) is another interesting topic that teachers can expound to course participants. Take care not to give the impression that all pretence is unethical in every circumstance.
- *Gang journalism* This is when reporters agree as a group what to publish or not to publish. The ethical issue is that the information agreed upon may turn out to be untrue or inaccurate.
- *Truth and objectivity* Teachers should begin with a general discussion about the difficulty of attaining absolute truth and objectivity in reporting. The angle that the reporter gives to the news is a subjective decision in which he or she tries to highlight certain fact(s) at the expense of others.

- *Accuracy and fairness* These are important ethical requirements in reporting, the meaning of which should be explained. Accuracy means a meticulous obsession with fine detail. For example, a reporter who misspells a source's name or gives a wrong figure as a statistic is not accurate. Fairness means giving the contending sides an equal hearing in reporting.

PHOTOJOURNALISM

This module would be incomplete without a section on photojournalism, including print media (newspapers and magazines) and broadcast media. It is important to explain to course participants the meaning of photojournalism: journalism based on telling the story in pictures, which may be still (newspapers and magazines) or film (video and television).

The main ethical issues that fall under the discussion of photojournalism include:

- *Faking of pictures* at the point of taking them and in processing;
- *Invasion of privacy* when taking the pictures;
- *Indecency*, which should be discussed within the cultural context, but is also affected by locale and time (for example, what is termed indecent now may not be so in five years' time, and what is indecent in Mozambique, may not be so in neighbouring Swaziland);
- *Human suffering* (e.g. sickness, accidents) should also be examined from the points of view about how a photojournalist should behave when taking such pictures, and how these should be treated for publication or broadcasting;
- *Death* – questions about how to take and publish pictures of the dead should be discussed both in the cultural and professional contexts; consideration should be taken not to hurt survivors;
- *Deceitful identification*, when photojournalists pose as people they are not in order to take pictures; and
- *Deportment (character and behaviour) of the photojournalist* should be discussed within the context of his or her relationship with people while taking the pictures.

Teachers should apply these topics to the particular media being discussed: print media or television. Each one has its own peculiar set of ethical problems, but there are also problems common to both.

It is not necessary, while discussing the problems peculiar to a particular medium, to separate the class (if it happens to be a mixed class) because by so doing, teachers would be depriving both groups of valuable information that they could use in their journalistic careers. In SADC countries, journalists sometimes switch from one particular medium to another. Newspaper journalists become television journalists and vice versa. Sometimes, former newspaper journalists head television stations and former television journalists head newspaper offices, particularly where 'political appointments' in government media are common.

COMMERCIALISM AND JOURNALISM ETHICS

Commercialisation of journalism refers to the preoccupation by the mass media and journalists on how to use the press to make money. This obsession often results in journalists and the mass media relegating the role of journalism and the mass media from working in the service of society to that of merely making money. Journalists become less sensitive to the need to serve the community by providing honest and truthful information.

Commercialism is more common in privately owned than government- or publicly-owned media. This is because the privately owned media use their commercial undertakings, particularly advertising, to support their media businesses. In other words, they have to make money in order to survive. In a fiercely competitive business world based on free enterprise, the battle for the survival of media houses can be very intense. The more intense the battle for survival by the private media, the more they use unorthodox, and often unethical, methods and ways of commercialisation and the less sensitive they become to the needs of the general public.

With the liberalisation of economies in Africa in the 1990s – which accompanied the advent of multiparty politics – the continent's government media also joined the commercialisation race so that African governments, which are constantly short of money, can hive them off from their subvention. A situation has, therefore, arisen in which the government media are also fighting for bigger circulations and greater advertising and other revenue-earning gimmicks just like the private media.

SENSATIONALISM

Sensationalism in reporting is one way in which the media, particularly newspapers, try to increase circulation. Sensationalism can be expressed in many ways. First, there is the deliberate exaggeration of the story to make it appear bigger than it really is. A few dead people become hundreds or even thousands; a dangerous disease breaking out in one district of a country is said to have broken out in the whole country; one corrupt minister in government becomes, in the story, the whole government being corrupt; one armed robbery in a city is reported as a 'spate of armed robberies'; one political party official who tells a lie grows into the whole political party being 'a party of liars'; one police officer accepting a bribe at a road block is reported as the whole police force conducting road blocks in order to receive bribes; part of the population being infected with HIV/AIDS becomes 'everyone in the country is infected with HIV/AIDS'; a few prostitutes in a backyard alley of a city are reported as hundreds of prostitutes invading the city; etc.

Headlines, in particular, are often used to make a story being reported sound sensational. One does not need to look very far to come across sensational headlines in Africa's newspapers, particularly the private tabloids. They are being used every day, literally screaming 'wolf' where there is merely a meek domestic cat; sources are made out to have said terrible things that they never actually said; they are quoted accurately, but taken completely out of context; fictitious sources are quoted; a big announcement is made, which is not supported by the story; etc.

Such sensationalism is often economically beneficial because it makes the curious public want to find out 'what happened' or 'is happening' or 'will happen' by buying the newspaper to read what is being reported. This is because nearly every newspaper in Africa is sold from the streets where such headlines are likely to attract buyers. Unfortunately, members of the public are cheated in the end because what is announced in the headline sometimes does not correspond to the real situation. When journalists and the media cheat people in this way, even for monetary gain, they are being unethical.

UNTRUTHFUL ADVERTISING

The media in Africa are falling prey to untruthful advertising which, again, they accept for the sake of money. Many advertisers, particularly those advertising consumer products or services, claim in their advertisements that their products are able to do this or that and the public responds to these claims by buying the products or services only to discover that they have been duped. Sometimes the advertisements deal with services that are either non-existent or are merely tricks.

Sometimes the effect of untruthful advertising is more serious than merely inconveniencing the people by telling them lies. Some of the advertisements actually harm the people. A typical case in Africa has been that of companies advertising tinned milk for babies, which UNICEF has proved to be responsible for the high rate of mortality of children under the age of five years because mothers have been feeding their babies this milk in unhygienic conditions. The bottles and teats have, in many cases, not been sterilised, resulting in many children suffering from the lethal diarrhoea.

The ethical responsibility of the media to the people with regard to advertisements that tell them lies or are harmful to the public is greater when those responsible for accepting and publishing the advertisements are aware of their untruthfulness and/or harmfulness. But media people are not free of blame even when they do not know that the advertisements could be lies or harmful. They need to take extra care to ensure that everything that is disseminated by their mass medium, including advertisements, is in the interest and benefit of the people and not against them.

THE TEACHER AND UNETHICAL COMMERCIALISATION OF THE MEDIA

As may have been deduced from the above discussion, commercialisation of the mass media does not lie completely in the hands of journalists. Non-journalists known as media advertising agents are also partly responsible from the advertising point of view. In this respect, commercialisation of the media as an ethical problem cannot be solved by merely teaching ethics to journalists. It also requires the teaching of advertising ethics to advertising agents and representatives who are responsible for placing the various advertisements in the media. This aspect, however, falls outside the ambit of this teaching guide.

There is, however, a lot to be said about commercialisation of the media and journalism as we have described it above (i.e. trying to promote the sale of media products by making them enticing to the people through the use of unethical means such as sensationalism).

The teacher here should discuss the two types of truthfulness in reporting and explain the ethical value of each of them. The two types of truthfulness in reporting include: 1. factual reporting that represents objective reality; and, 2. factual reporting that truthfully and accurately relays what the source said.

The teacher should begin by laying the philosophical foundation of journalism and the media. The media are there to provide people with the information they need to adjust their interaction with the changing environment. The information the media report should, therefore, be true i.e. represent objective reality. Otherwise, the people will make false adjustments by trying to cope with or deal with a situation that is not there. This cheating by journalists and the media is not only bad because it makes the people look like fools, but it is also bad because journalists and the media have broken their sacred trust with the people by providing them with truthful information.

OBJECTIVE REALITY

Journalists owe it to the public to report things that are objectively true, although this is not always possible, given the often little time reporters have to check on the facts they are reporting. When, however, journalists do not make an effort to try to check whether what they are reporting corresponds to objective reality, when they have good reason to doubt its truthfulness, they are acting unethically. This is also the case when they know that what they are reporting does not correspond to the objective reality but still go ahead and report it. This is the reason why journalists are supposed to cross-check what sources are telling them with other sources to ensure that what they finally report corresponds to the objective reality.

In Africa, what this writer calls 'vendetta journalism' has been widely practised. This is the type of reporting in which journalists know that what they are reporting is untrue but still go ahead and report it so that they square up or hurt their enemy who is the subject of the news. 'Vendetta journalism' is clearly unethical.

REPORTING SOURCES

Journalists are required by the ethical tenet to report accurately what their sources tell them. When they report inaccurately or construct blatant lies, they can be said to report untruthfully. The untruthfulness here refers to inaccurately reporting what a source actually says as opposed to whether or not what the source told them represents objective truth. In other words, journalists have an ethical obligation to report exactly what they have been told, without adding or subtracting anything. They should also report what they have been told in its proper and rightful context and not out of context.

Journalists, however, also have a duty to ensure that what they are reporting as having been said by the source, corresponds to the objective reality i.e. is objectively true. Where journalists know or have good reason to doubt the truthfulness (in terms of objective reality) of what the source has told them, they have an ethical duty to cross-check with other sources so that they can help establish the truth by exposing to the public the information the other sources are giving on the issue. Journalists behave unethically when, knowing that a source has not told them the truth, they still go ahead and report it without providing the public with additional information from other sources.

The teacher should give examples showing what consequences untruthful reporting can have for people. Dramatic but real examples drive the point much more forcefully to the learners. For instance, one could give the example of a newspaper that falsely reports that there is a coup in the country. The teacher can then proceed to give instances of how the general public is likely to behave in response to such a report. Wanton destruction, looting, unruly celebrations, soldiers shooting, people dying, and people in government and their families living in fear could be some of the consequences of such a report. At the end of it all, life would have been disturbed so much that some indelible (physical or mental) scars would remain with many members of the general public.

With examples such as this one, it will become absolutely clear that it is highly immoral for journalists and media houses to make money from such unnecessary and uncalled-for alarming of the people. But even with less dramatic examples, it is possible for the teacher to drive the point home to the learners that sensationalism in reporting is morally wrong. The surprising thing, and this is what the teacher needs to emphasise, is that the mass media in Africa are carrying out sensational reporting every day and society lets them go scot-free. Should society not take journalists and the media to task for violating a sacred trust if they do not supply people with truthful and correct information? The positive answer to this question should in turn invite suggestions from the class about what African society can do to prevent journalists and the media from making fools of them by sensa-tionalising what they report to the point of falsifying it and, therefore, making life difficult for them.

Another equally effective approach is to make the class, consisting of journalists, objectively discuss the issue with regard to themselves. Would they write, edit and publish or disseminate sensationalised stories for the sake of money and competition? Ask each member of the class to be very frank in discussing this subject. The pull for making more money can and does often outweigh ethical and moral principles. It is a temptation to which journalists and media houses succumb quite often, without much thought. Asking them to give it some thought may make them just a little more careful before they act.

INCREASING PRICES OF MEDIA PRODUCTS

There is another type of commercialism in the African media which is taking place in many countries in the face of increasing inflation: many media houses are increasing the prices of their media products in order to make more money. Take the prices of newspapers as an example. The prices of many newspapers have trebled in many African countries over a period of less than ten years. Consequently, it costs a newspaper reader who buys one daily newspaper everyday in some countries, such as Zambia, about half of his or her monthly salary.

When newspaper owners fail to make the 75–80% revenue they are supposed to from advertising, they try to make it from newspaper sales by increasing the price astronomically. This writer was at one time on the Board of Directors of one such newspaper in Zambia and his pleas for the owners of the newspaper not to unnecessarily increase the price of the newspaper always fell on deaf ears.

The other forms of commercialisation of the media, such as stunts, crusades and promotions have never been common among the African press and should, therefore, not worry the teacher. Of more concern should be the fairly widespread use of supplements and inserts. Most of the supplement publications to newspapers have occurred when there are special events such as independence anniversary celebrations or agriculture and commercial fairs or shows. The practice is to ask companies and organisations to send congratulatory messages or write-ups which are paid for and which mostly fill the newspaper supplement. The remaining space is used up by promotional features about the same companies and organisations that have placed advertisements in the supplement.

The only ethical problem that arises from these supplements is that of sometimes not making a clear difference between promotional write-ups in feature form on the one hand and advertisements on the other. Quite often the two are treated in almost the same way in a given supplement. Because they are paid for, advertisements in newspapers, including special supplements, should always be distinguished i.e. set aside from write-ups or features about companies or organisations that are being advertised. It would, of course, be immoral for a newspaper to ask for payment from a company or organisation for a write-up or feature published in a supplement because these are not advertisements *per se*.

With regards to newspaper inserts that often take the form of the so-called shopping guides, these are, strictly speaking, publications from other companies or organisations which the newspaper company agrees to circulate together with its newspaper. The newspaper is, therefore, not liable for the contents, although it should generally be in agreement with the general import of the contents of the insert. In other words, it does not help the newspaper's image if it distributes inserts that, for example, contradict its editorial policy. For example, if the newspaper policy is not to support freemasons, it would be morally wrong for it to distribute an insert about freemasons.

ADVERTISING

As suggested above, the most commonly used forms of commercialisation of the press is that of advertising. Advertising is the promotion of goods, services or any personal sentiments in the media in return for payment. There are many ethical issues that come with advertising and we will deal with the main ones here.

- *Advertising that encourages dishonesty and/or crime*
  When advertising encourages dishonesty and/or criminal behaviour, it becomes ethically unacceptable. For example, a newspaper should not advertise the loss of some valuable item (e.g. a watch) and offer a reward of money to whoever comes forward with it unless there is a note in the same advertisement that this (the bringing of the lost item and the payment of appreciation) must be done through the police. Otherwise criminals and dishonest people may be encouraged to steal the item so that they can be 'rewarded' by the payment. The teacher should explain that some ethical offences also become criminal offences in some cases. This should not lead us to conclude that all ethical offences are also criminal or civil offences at law. Ethics is completely different from law.

- *Advertisements that are contrary to the values and principles of the media house*
  Advertisements that are contrary to the values and principles of the media house as expressed in its editorial policy and similar guidelines compromise another class of ethical issues with which advertising is concerned. The best example this author can give of this phenomenon is a situation where a newspaper, like the *National Mirror* in Zambia, which is jointly owned by Protestant churches and the Catholic Church, published soothsaying advertisements. The advertisements were withdrawn as soon as this author, who was doing research in the press in Zambia at the newspaper's offices, reminded the media house's Executive Director that what they were doing was unethical, according to their own Christian principles and beliefs that only God can foretell

the future. To use another example, it would not be ethical for a Catholic newspaper or radio station to advertise the use of condoms as a way to fight the spread of HIV, when the church that owns the newspaper preaches that the use of condoms is immoral. In other words, it is immoral for a mass medium to carry advertisements for things that the same medium has publicly condemned as being wrongful, simply because they want to make money. The principal at play here is that it is immoral to make money by advertising things that you consider are wrong or bad. It is not so much what is being advertised that matters, but rather the moral stand of the mass medium, as represented by the people operating it, on what is being advertised. This is what the teacher should stress to the course participants. In conclusion, it is important for anybody teaching the effect of commercialism on the ethical performance of media houses to first establish the philosophical base that it is morally wrong to put the making of money before service to individual persons and the community at large. Journalism is there first and foremost as a service to people and not purely as a business venture to make it possible for cunning individuals to make money.

CULTURE AND JOURNALISM ETHICS

Culture may simply be defined as a 'way of life'. Every people has a particular way of living: of doing things and of behaviour based on their values (things they look up to), principles (guiding pronouncements in life) and norms (behavioural precepts).

If journalism is about serving a particular people's mass communication needs, then it must take into account and operate within that particular people's cultural setting, which should include observing their ethical norms, values and principles in order to be effective.

African culture is rich in ethical communicative norms, values and principles, some of which journalists in Africa should observe, in addition to the journalistic norms bequeathed to them from the Euro-American journalistic tradition that accompanied the introduction of journalism into Africa.

The teacher using these guidelines should know the basic tenets of African ethical values and norms, values and principles if he or she is to teach the relevance and applicability of African culture to journalism ethics for African journalists. What follows are some broad outlines.

FOUNDATIONS OF AFRICAN ETHICS

The essence of African morality is that it is more societal than spiritual. It is more 'dynamic' than 'static'. For many Africans, a person is what he or she is because of what he or she does rather than doing what he or she does because of what he or she is. In other words, 'goodness' in a human being is not something abstract but something concrete. To demonstrate the concreteness of 'goodness' or 'badness' in a person, Africans attribute these qualities to parts of the body. For instance, 'kindness' is placed in the heart. So is 'cruelty'. A person is said to have a 'kind' heart, while another is said to have a 'cruel' heart.

Like people from other continents, Africans believe that 'good' people can build a community while 'bad' people can destroy it. It is, therefore, the duty of members of the community to help reform the 'bad' people, where this is possible. For Africans, people can be bad in two ways. First, a person can be bad because he or she is possessed by bad spirits or is brought up in a 'bad' family. These types of bad people cannot be reformed by society. Second, there is an equally strong belief that individuals in society can be bad because they want to be or are being influenced by friends and/or relatives. Traditional African societies try to rehabilitate such people. The practice of mutual correction is an acceptable practice in which it is considered the responsibility of everyone in the community to try to reform them so that they can be useful to the community whose survival depends on their contribution.

The biggest problem in journalism ethics in Africa today does not lie in passing on ethical knowledge to the journalists, important as this may be. It lies in ensuring that journalists adhere to the ethical norms, values and principles in their profession. In this respect, the teacher would do well to remind the people he or she is training to take a leaf from the African cultural tradition of collective ethical correction. This would be achieved at two levels.

The first level is that of journalists as a professional community who should, in the true African spirit, each work indefatigably at mutually correcting one another whenever one falters ethically.

The second level is that of the general public who should also keep an eye on journalistic performance and draw journalists to what they see as unethical behaviour so that the journalists can serve them better. But for the general public to be able to do this, it needs to be educated on what constitutes unethical behaviour in journalism. There is, clearly, a need to sensitise the public on what should be its expectations regarding the duties and responsibilities of journalists and the media to it. The role of giving the public this type of education falls on the shoulders of journalists and media houses.

VIRTUES IN AFRICAN ETHICS

Apart from taking a leaf from the communal corrective approach of African ethics, African journalism can also profit by emulating some of the virtues Africans have traditionally looked for in a virtuous person. There are many such virtues and the teacher is advised to look into his or her own ethnic (tribal) tradition rather than merely discuss the few that this author is raising here for the simple reason that the list given in these guidelines is not exhaustive.

SELF-RESPECT

In African etiquette, a human person or *umuntu*, should have self-respect in everything he or she does. This is one of the most distinguishing characteristics by which *umuntu* is distinguished from an animal. *Umuntu* respects himself or herself in all that he or she does so that he or she can proudly tell others what he or she did without feeling ashamed. When *umuntu* is ashamed to tell others of what he or she did, then it is a sign that he or she is acting unethically.

One tribe in Zambia, the Lozi, have a word for self-respect: *likute*. A person without *likute*, they would say, behaves unbecomingly and is not fit to live in a community. The teacher can find similar expressions in his or her language to express the same thing. The author has always found it useful to ask the class to come up with expressions from their own languages to express *likute* or similar sentiments.

Journalists, the teacher should point out, should also have self-respect in all that they do. If they have *likute*, it will be almost impossible for them to accept bribes, which are perhaps one of the biggest ethical problems on the continent. A journalist who has *likute* will not report lies or put words in the mouth of a source etc. The teacher here has a very rich repertoire of journalistic unethical behaviour that is an affront to self-respect on which he or she can peg not one, but a series of lessons on the need for *likute* in African journalism.

BEING BRAVE AND PERSEVERING

Africans have traditionally admired bravery and despised cowardice. African folklore is full of fireside tragedies, told with great relish, in which the most beautiful maiden is always given in marriage to a brave warrior who, for instance, kills a marauding animal such as a lion. A brave person who kills a dangerous snake is always eulogised and sung in songs of praise. So is one who ends up being killed by the dangerous animal he or she is trying to eliminate in order to ensure the safety of the community.

Here again, the ethics teacher can draw lessons from journalistic practice in Africa where cowardice has become more common than acts of bravery. Scores of African journalists, particularly those working for government media, are afraid to tell the truth for fear of being in trouble with government. They fear being detained, dismissed, physically attacked, etc., and compromise their ethical responsibilities by reporting lies so that they are not punished by the authorities for telling the truth.

Unlike African traditional ethics, however, journalists who are cowards are not always condemned by either their fellow journalists or society as a whole. On the contrary, they are sometimes even paid glowing tribute as being people who are true patriots (and matriots) 'working for national unity and development'. The teacher should solicit examples from the class.

RESPECT FOR SENIORITY

Traditionally, Africans respect age and rank. Elderly people have a very special place in society because it is generally assumed that their life experiences are a reservoir of wisdom from which the young can learn. They are, therefore, accorded priority in everything, including the right to speak. There are numerous ways in which young people show respect to the elderly or high-ranking people in the community. The teacher may want to mention some of these, particularly those akin to the journalistic profession. An example that comes to mind is criticising or disapproving of what elders have done or are doing. Some people do not allow their respect for elders or those who hold positions of authority to prevent them from expressing their disapproval or criticisms. However, one has to choose the right words.

Journalism today, particularly that practised in the private press, can learn from this approach. Here the teacher can draw examples from private newspapers that have criticised people in government. Let the class discuss whether the editorials contravene the idea of being respectful to elders or people in authority. Even the way journalists ask questions should show some respect. For example, while Nelson Mandela was on a Far East state visit in his capacity as South African President, a reporter (who was not an African) asked him when he was going to marry Graca Machel (who was at his side). Mandela deflected the question by saying: 'Young man, in Africa where I come from, young men like you cannot ask me such a question because I am as good as your grandfather.' The teacher could create a discussion about whether Mandela was right in referring to Africa in this way.

ETHICAL THINKING

Ethical behaviour should be part of our lives and not just something we draw on when it is convenient to do so. Africa's journalists should think and live like Africans and not like Europeans or Americans. A person cannot take his or her culture's ethical tenets seriously by leading a life alien to that culture. In this respect, the attitude to African culture of many young journalists in Africa is a source of worry. Many young reporters look down on Africa's culture and imitate as well as emulate the culture of Europe and America. This is not only evident in their behaviour, but also in their thought processes and in the way they speak – French, English and Portuguese being the lingua franca. To be able to speak a foreign language is often regarded as being 'more civilised'. Those who speak local languages are often looked down upon, which has resulted in many young people being unable to speak their mother tongue.

Apart from speech, the behaviour of many young people in Africa, including reporters, is also foreign. Fast disappearing are the days when Africa's youth sat down with their grandparents at the fireside to listen to stories or exchange inspiring and intellectually stimulating sayings, idioms and axioms. Africa's oral literature is declining so fast that, within the next few decades, it is likely to be reduced to the bare minimum or possibly disappear.

The author does not believe in the superiority of one culture over another as many of Africa's youths seem to suggest by word or deed. He does not believe in development being defined as the moving away from traditional cultures to modernity, where modernity is defined as consisting of foreign ways of doing things. But he does believe that cultural traditions and practices that have outlived their usefulness should be discarded ... and replaced not necessarily by foreign ones or their adaptations, but by locally inspired forms of such cultural traditions and practices. He also believes in the preservation of those cultural aspects that are still useful and valuable to the African society. The mistake many youths are making, particularly those in urban centres, is the indiscriminate discarding of African cultural traditions and practices, irrespective of their current value to society.

Unless journalists on the African continent learn to observe cultural traditions and practices, it does not make much sense to emphasise the application of African ethical values to their journalistic profession.

THE ROLE OF THE TEACHER

The teacher has the somewhat daunting task of encouraging journalists participating in his or her journalism ethics course to start applying African cultural values, principles and norms to the way they practice journalism in particular and their philosophy of life generally.

First and foremost, he or she needs a class that consists of journalists who believe in the importance of living and thinking 'African'. Should the teacher find that his or her class is full of *evolues* – as the French call Africans whose lives closely imitate French culture – he or she has the task of inculcating in them the pride of being African. Only then can the transition of applying African culture to the journalistic profession be made easier.

The teacher might find it better to use the method of peer pressure by identifying journalists who strongly believe in their African heritage and conducting a series of debates and seminars on the topic. It may also be useful to bring to the class a family that leads a typical African cultural life and another that leads a life of *evolues* and encourage the two to interact for a day or two with the course participants.

Attempting to change people's cultural pathways is not a one-day or few weeks' job. It is a life commitment that may be sparked during a training session. The teacher and the class should, therefore, work out ways and means of ensuring that experiences are shared with course participants long after they have left the course. Some kind of networking should be arranged so that the journalists can monitor each other's progress.

It is ironic that some Africans need to be almost coerced into remaining African – not only in name, but also in behaviour. So strong is the pull of Euro-American cultural traditions and practices, which the world media have made to look like they represent 'world culture'. Under normal circumstances, a person does not need to be coerced. In this regard, it is worth observing that the experience of Africa has been such that African culture has been strongest in countries where people have been encouraged to maintain their own identity.

In countries where there was a policy of 'assimilation', such as in French and Portuguese Africa, and where Africans had a chance of becoming 'French or Portuguese people', there was a craving by the African *evolues* tired of being 'European' to show the Europeans that they belonged to a different culture. Some of the *evolues*, however, were happy to be 'French or Portuguese people' and did not want to give up either the practice or the idea. On the other hand, in African colonies where the colonialists imposed separate development between Europeans and Africans, Africans developed the attitude and practice of maintaining their own way of life and leaving European cultural traditions alone. This is one of the reasons why the practice of European culture is generally stronger among Africans living in former French, Portuguese and Belgian colonies than it is among those belonging to former English or German colonies. However, this does not mean there are no 'black Europeans' in the former English and German colonies.

LANGUAGE AND CULTURE

There is a close relationship between the language that journalists in Africa use and their ability to practise journalism as Africans. The language in use often dictates the cultural, and hence, ethical environment of the journalist. When journalists are subjected to operating in a foreign language, as they are quite often in Africa, their thinking and behaviour tends to be in line with that language. The use of the English, French and Portuguese languages in the African media, therefore, has not encouraged African journalists to observe African ethical tenets. In some cases, journalists, depending upon their competency in the foreign language, tend to think like the owners of that language. Thus, their philosophical and ethical outlook tends to be foreign rather than African.

The author is not suggesting that media that operate in the former colonial languages should be done away with. On the contrary, they should be kept, because they play a very useful role in the communication set-up of a continent which, without these languages, would find it very difficult to communicate to all its peoples. But it does mean that African journalists, while operating in these languages, should also use their mother tongues, to keep in touch with African etiquette. This can then translate into desirable ethical behaviour in the practice of journalism. It also means that African journalists who are 'fortunate' enough to work as journalists in media that use local languages should be proud of using their languages to communicate to the public through the mass media. The situation where journalists working for the vernacular media believe they are lesser journalists than those working for the English, French or Portuguese media should not arise. In this connection, the author admires Tanzanian journalists who operate in Swahili, as well as Afrikaans-speaking journalists in South Africa.

Let's look at an example which illustrates the fact that using the local language in media forces journalists to ethically think and behave like the users of the particular language. During the 1980s, while conducting a rural newspaper workshops in Sereje, central Zambia, the author witnessed an occasion when a journalist was forced to translate his or her journalism into the behavioural pattern of the owners of the language being used. While editing a laboratory workshop newspaper in Lala, the language of the people in the area, workshop participants were involved in an argument about a headline they were to use: '*ba Kaunda bafika*' or '*Kaunda afika*'. Both headlines have the same meaning: 'Kaunda arrives'. The first is plural and, hence, Lala respectable form, while the second, which is singular, is regarded as disrespectful. After a very long argument, the workshop participants agreed to use the longer but respectful version. It is important to mention here that had the workshop participants decided to be faithful to the Anglo-American headline style, they would have opted for the less wordy headline.

The teacher can lead the class to think of similar examples where journalistic behaviour is dictated by the moral values, principles and norms of the language being used. The teacher should not shun the heated discussion that is likely to accompany the examples participants will give. In some cases, the issue may not even be resolved by the end of the class or workshop, but there is value in having course participants spend some time thinking about such issues. They are bound to be resolved later, particularly if they are key to the journalistic operations of those who are raising them.

The teacher should emphasise that journalists who operate in local languages should also think in those languages. There is a big difference in the ethical approach of a journalist who thinks in English, French or Portuguese, but writes a news story in his or her mother tongue, and one who both thinks and writes in the same language.

It is important that journalists who operate in a local African language write their news stories or do other journalistic productions in that language rather than first write in English, French or Portuguese and merely translate it into the local language.

CROSS-CULTURAL JOURNALISTIC
ETHICAL BEHAVIOUR

Whereas the author may sound as if he condones the compartmentalisation of journalism ethics in Africa, this would be most impractical to the profession. Journalism is universal and should, therefore, share ethical values from country to country and from people to people.

There is certainly room for universal ethical values, norms and principles in journalism, but these should, indeed, be universal and not national or racial values, norms and principles which certain nations present as universal. In other words, they should stand the test of universalism by being acceptable to all journalists worldwide after taking into account their own cultural values, norms and principles.

One of the issues of journalism as a profession in Africa has been the general acceptance of principles brought to the continent by those from the North.

Many appear to have absorbed everything about journalism without discriminating which of the values, norms and principles are valid in the African situation and should, therefore, be adopted and which ones should be adapted or discarded.

The teacher should emphasise that journalism has to be contextualised in African culture while having its roots in the universally accepted values, norms, principles and philosophy of the profession. Journalism cannot serve its society unless it reflects its culture – particularly its values, norms and principles.

THE TEACHER AND RESEARCH IN CULTURE

There appears to be a need to infuse African ethics, including African morality, in journalism in Africa. Whether African journalists see this need is another question. The teacher can help students see this by stressing that journalism in Africa will only start to truly serve the needs of the African people by being responsive to and respecting their value systems.

Assuming, however, that the majority of African journalists agree on the need to inculcate African ethics in the continent's journalism, the teacher still has an obligation to help translate this belief into action. He or she can, among other things, teach students how to apply certain African moral values in journalism and what the likely effects would be. But the teacher cannot do this effectively unless he or she is sure of what the moral values are. This can only come about if the teacher carries out ongoing research in African moral values and how they can be applied to journalism. To the author's knowledge, hardly any such research is being carried out in Africa.

Research needs to be conducted on African morality and how it can be applied to journalism. Yet, for some reason, scholars have not been active in this particular type of research. Journalism schools have generally been without the resources or funding to support such research. However, scholars in journalism schools, particularly universities, could write proposals to conduct such research and their institutions, or any other funders, should attempt to source money to sponsor such projects.

Many practising journalists have shown a lack of interest in researching African morality as it applies to journalism in Africa. Few journalists in the typical newsroom would even want to talk about the issue, dismissing it as an academic exercise for people in tertiary education institutions and not for busy journalists who have to search for news and prepare it for dissemination within strict deadlines. What they forget or do not seem to understand is that the issue of African morality being made applicable to their everyday journalistic chores has the potential of making their work not only easier but also more acceptable to the people they are supposed to serve. As pointed out earlier in this guide, this lack of interest in issues concerning journalism ethics is certainly due to the lack of, or insufficient exposure to, the subject in their training.

By merely teaching the subject of African morality and journalism ethics in Africa, the teacher is not only helping to raise interest in the subject (so that some research can be undertaken, which will contribute to the effective teaching of the subject), but is also helping to make African journalism more effective by making it more applicable to the African situation. Herein lies the importance of introducing the issue of African morality and its applicability to journalism ethics in Africa in this course. African journalism cannot ignore Africa's approach to morality and be effective. It is bound to continue being, by and large, a foreign means of communication, which Africa has merely adopted and not adapted.

CONCLUSION

Journalism ethics is an important and necessary component of the journalism courses. Without ethical considerations, journalism becomes an activity without any purpose; merely a trade and not a profession. Ethical considerations give journalism meaning and direction, and places the service of people and society at the centre of its activities.

One of the dangers facing journalism today is that it is moving away from serving society to being a purely commercial venture. Those involved in the industry have become more interested in the opportunities it offers to make money than in its potential to contribute to the betterment of the human situation. When journalism is seen only as a business undertaking, ethical rules are usually discarded; when money is only what matters, then journalism truly loses direction.

Stating that journalism is a service to the community does not mean that it serves a clique of people holding political power. Unfortunately, this is what some journalism has become in African countries where governments are still holding on to government-owned and -controlled media. Such journalism sidesteps the real needs of the people in favour of political ambitions. There is no problem if such journalism is funded and supported by the political parties themselves, but there is a problem when the people it is ignoring provide funding through taxes. It is immoral for African governments to use public funds to support personal political ambitions. Herein lies the biggest argument against the existence of government-owned and -controlled media in Africa.

Teaching modules

Course objectives

By the end of this course on journalism ethics, course participants should:

- understand the meaning of journalism ethics and its close relation to freedom of the press;
- understand why it is important that journalists practise their profession ethically;
- understand ethical principles and values, and be able to apply them in solving problems in journalism ethics;
- know how to deal with ethical issues in journalism posed by government, employers, the behaviour of the journalist, and the demands of society; and
- understand the roles of journalists and the media in society.

Course content and method of teaching

This course is designed to span a period of three weeks. It is taught in conjunction with other courses mentioned in the first section of the Teacher's Guide. Eleven sessions are planned, comprising four sessions in one full day (preferably the second day of the particular course being offered), five sessions in the second week and two sessions in the final week.

Teachers should keep in mind that not all of the sessions are of equal length. The four sessions in one full day are divided as follows: 08:30 to 10:00; 10:30 to 12:30; 14:00 to 15:00; and 15:30 to 16:30. In the second week, the time slot should be 10:30 to 12:30 every day for five days. In the final week, the same time slot should be taken for two days. It is recommended that these days be towards the end of the course.

MODULE 1: INTRODUCTION TO JOURNALISM ETHICS

AIM

The main aim of this module is to give the course participants a theoretical base for understanding and applying journalism ethics.

OBJECTIVES

By the end of the sessions, course participants should:
- understand the meaning of journalism ethics and its close relation to freedom of the press;
- understand why it is important that journalists practise their profession ethically;
- understand ethical principles and values, and be able to apply them in solving problems in journalism ethics.

CONTENT

- General theoretical background, including:
  - a definition of press freedom;
  - a definition of democracy and how it is linked to a free press; and
  - a discussion about the role of the press in a democracy.
- Ethics in general, and media and journalism ethics in particular;
- A historical perspective of journalism ethics in Europe;
- The development of media ideologies;
- The challenge of communication developments.

SESSION 1: A GENERAL THEORETICAL BACKGROUND TO JOURNALISM ETHICS

By the end of this session, course participants should be able to:
- define press freedom;
- define democracy and explain its relation to freedom of the press; and
- demonstrate an understanding of the role of the press in a democracy.

Content
- Press freedom
- Democracy
- Press freedom and democracy

Teaching activity
Teachers should progress from the known to the unknown by first asking the course participants to define these terms and then working on correcting their definitions if these are inaccurate. This enables the course participants to think about the issues as the session progresses. They are more likely to remember what they have thought about than what teachers tell them as a matter of course.

SESSION 2: ETHICS IN GENERAL AND MEDIA AND JOURNALISM ETHICS IN PARTICULAR

By the end of this session, course participants should be able to:
- demonstrate an understanding of human ethics in general;
- demonstrate an understanding of professional ethics in general;
- demonstrate an understanding of journalism ethics; and
- be able to narrate briefly how journalism ethics developed in Europe with the advent of journalism as we know it today.

Content
- The importance of ethics in society
- Ethics for professional people and bodies
- Journalism ethics
- History of journalism ethics in Europe

Teaching activity
This session should be taught in a straightforward lecture format, allowing time for questions and clarification.

SESSION 3: DEVELOPMENT OF MEDIA IDEOLOGIES

By the end of this session, course participants should be able to:
- demonstrate an understanding of the neo-multiparty theory of the press (Kasoma), paying particular application to its ethical implications for journalism in Africa;
- demonstrate an understanding of the four theories of the press (Siebert, et al.) and their bearing on global journalism ethics; and
- identify any other theory of the press and demonstrate how it can be applied to journalism ethics.

Content
- The neo-multiparty theory of the press
- The four theories of the press
- Any other theory of the press

Teaching activity
This session should be taught in a straightforward lecture format, allowing time for questions and clarification.

Session 4: The challenge of communication developments

By the end of this session, course participants should be able to:
- understand the ethical challenges posed by new communication technologies;
- understand the ethical challenges posed by the use of computers, with particular reference to the Internet; and
- understand the concept of the global village and its ethical challenges.

Content
- New communication technologies and their ethical challenges
- Computer-mediated mass communication and its ethical challenges
- The global village and its ethical challenges

Teaching activity
This session should be taught in a straightforward lecture format, allowing time for questions and clarification.

Module 2: Ethical framework of media law

Aim

The main aim of this module is to enable course participants to understand the relationship between journalism ethics and journalism law.

Objectives

By the end of the sessions, course participants should be able to:
- differentiate between journalism ethics and journalism law;
- differentiate between restrictive journalism laws and enabling journalism laws; and
- understand clearly what defamation is in ethics.

Content

- Journalism ethics and journalism law
- Defamation

Session 5: Journalism ethics and media law

By the end of this session, course participants should be able to:
- understand why journalism ethics should not normally be enforced by law;
- understand the difference between journalism ethics and media law;
- understand the difference between enabling and restrictive journalism laws;
- understand the concepts of the right to know and the right to access information;
- understand how the Official Secrets Act works against press freedom; and
- understand how Law and Order (Maintenance) Acts reduce press freedom.

Content
- Enforcement of journalism ethics by law as an exception
- The difference between journalism ethics and media law
- Enabling journalism laws, such as those of freedom of information

- The right to know and access to information
- The Official Secrets Act
- The Law and Order (Maintenance) Act

Teaching activity

This session should be taught in a straightforward lecture format, allowing time for questions and clarification.

Session 6: Defamation

By the end of this session, course participants should be able to:
- understand defamation as an ethical requirement;
- state how defamation can be prevented; and
- state the traditional defences of defamation.

Content
- Defamation as an ethical requirement
- How to prevent defamation
- Traditional defences of defamation

Teaching activity

This session should be taught in a straightforward lecture format, allowing time for questions and clarification.

Session 7: Honouring confidences

By the end of this session, course participants should be able to:
- understand the general requirement to reveal sources in journalism;
- understand the meaning of journalistic confidences as exceptions;
- understand how journalists should arrive at promising not to reveal a source;
- know how to use the various formulae describing a source not named; and
- understand the consequences of breaking the promise of not revealing a source.

Content
- Importance of sources in reporting
- How to treat sources in reporting
- Understanding the various types of confidences in reporting
- The use and meaning of various formulae used to mask the identity of sources

Teaching activity
This session should be taught in a straightforward lecture format, allowing time for questions and clarification.

SESSION 8: THE THREE CARDINAL ETHICAL REQUIREMENTS OF REPORTING THE TRUTH FAIRLY AND ACCURATELY

By the end of this session, course participants should be able to:
• understand the meaning of truth reporting;
• understand the meaning of fairness in reporting; and
• understand the meaning of accuracy in reporting.

Content
• The two meanings of truth in reporting
• The meaning of fairness in reporting
• The meaning of accuracy in reporting

Teaching activity
This session should be taught in a straightforward lecture format, allowing time for questions and clarification.

SESSION 9: SENSATIONALISM

By the end of this session, course participants should be able to:
• understand the meaning of sensationalism in reporting;
• understand why sensationalism in reporting is ethically unacceptable; and
• understand the meaning of objective reporting.

Content
• Commercialism and sensationalism
• Objective reporting

Teaching activity
This session should be taught in a straightforward lecture format, allowing time for questions and clarification.

SESSION 10: AFRICAN MORALITY AND JOURNALISM ETHICS

By the end of this session, course participants should be able to:
- explain the foundations of African morality;
- explain the relationship of some of the African ethical values to journalism ethics; and
- apply African ethical values from their own tribe to journalism ethics.

Content
- Foundations of African morality
- Application of African moral values to journalism ethics

Teaching activity
This session should be taught in a straightforward lecture format, allowing time for questions and clarification.

SESSION 11: ENFORCEMENT OF JOURNALISM ETHICS

By the end of this session, course participants should be able to:
- understand that journalism ethics cannot be enforced by law;
- understand how journalism ethics can be enforced at the journalist's personal level;
- understand how journalism ethics can be enforced at the media house level; and
- understand how journalism ethics can be enforced at the journalists' association level.

Content
- Reasons why journalism ethics cannot be enforced by law
- Censorship
- Personal commitment by the journalist to observe journalism ethics
- The media house and the enforcement of journalism ethics
- The journalists' association and the enforcement of journalism ethics

Teaching activity
This session should be taught in a straightforward lecture format, allowing time for questions and clarification.

INDEX